D0898029

CONSTITUTIONAL FUNCTION OF PRESIDENTIAL-ADMINISTRATIVE SEPARATION

Henry J. Merry

University Press of America™

PREFACE

Jimmy Carter's first years in the White House provided a rare opportunity in the political science education of many Americans. We could see as seldom before that the presidency is a matter of few attainments and many frustrations. The voters in 1976 had elected a man with firm determination to set right a host of disturbing things and the sparse performance record made us think anew about the difficulties of government. Jimmy Carter was an outsider; but that was far from the whole story. Political science analysts have said for decades that any president spends two years learning the ropes. Presidents Johnson and Ford found that their long experience as congressional leaders did not prepare them fully for life in the Oval Office. All presidents have been circumscribed by counterforces. Those who seemed less obstructed were less determined to make changes. The difficulties were more in the system than in the man. The educational challenge of the Carter contrast was the added reason to probe a long growing question, that is, what is the constitutional essence of the mixed inner relationships of our complex system of elected and appointed officials. More particularly, we need to ascertain how far the presidency must share types of functions with coordinate political and governmental institutions.

Presidents have a wide choice of roles but they can act effectively on only a few selected matters. A president who wishes to supervise a particular operation must take the time and effort to master the specialized details. That can be done in but a few situations. Even then, it may disturb higher responsibilities, such as guiding general policies and keeping prepared for a sudden crisis. Most specialized policy must be made at the subunit levels of administration and legislation. My interest in this subject began thirty years ago when I was a fifth level official trying to please both a liberal assistant department secretary and a conservative congressional subcommittee.

The boundary between the presidential few and the subunit many is neither official nor systematic but it is substantial and persistent. In large part, it may reflect an external/internal contrast. Presidents find that they have a freer hand for dramatic action on the more strictly foreign affairs issues. When matters are mixed, such as the energy program, the more the domestic involvement, the greater the difficulty. President Carter intended to stress domestic projects. He first sought the "moral equivalent of war" in a restrictive energy-tax proposal. But personal diplomacy soon seemed more attractive and he found the moral equivalent in the human rights goal of world wide freedom for published

i

political dissent. That crusade gave the liberal press and public grounds for moral pride in the nation despite the meagre domestic record. He also made clearer the presidential emphasis on public relations—press conferences, television talks, and circuit appearances. Public political prestige depends more upon impressions outside of Washington than upon relationships with the houses of Congress and the administrative units. Americans seem to prefer that a president be chief citizen more than chief administrator.

The presidential involvement in external relationships is matched by bureaucratic domination of most internal governmental matters. Government organization charts may indicate vertical lines of control from the president down through a structural pyramid. But political science analysts are almost unanimous that executive branch unity is a lot more myth than fact. Department and agency heads serve several masters in addition to the White House. Many heads are also new to their posts and they rely heavily upon career officials. These last tend to respond horizontally more than vertically. Many appointed officials also engage extensively in congressionally authorized legislation and adjudication. Logically, they look to committees of Congress and the courts even more than to higher executives. Another compounding development is that presidents increasingly depend more upon their Executive Office staffs and their inner circle advisers than upon the cabinet and subcabinet. President Carter hoped to reverse that trend, but it persists.

Political scientists differ on their characterizations of the executive branch division. The most helpful terms seem to be "presidential government" and "permanent government." The latter includes thousands of career policy makers. Whether this presidential-administrative separation is constitutionally functional or dysfunctional became a problem for me when I taught political science at Purdue University and it has been my main retirement interest. This book examines the legitimacy of the existing semiautonomous administrative force with particular attention to its involvement in specialized legislative and judicial functions and to its responsiveness to Congress and the courts as well as to higher executives. The hope is that this explanation of the constitutional pattern of complex operations may assist university students and others in understanding American national government.

Ann Arbor, Michigan   February 1978

CONSTITUTIONAL FUNCTION

OF PRESIDENTIAL-ADMINISTRATIVE SEPARATION

CONTENTS

Contents

INTRODUCTION

The basic question which this book considers is whether Americans should be disturbed constitutionally about the confusing pattern of specialized operations in the United States government. The familiar three branch model, in which Congress, the presidency, and the courts, are supposed to exercise separately legislative, executive and judicial powers, is often less descriptive of the government than an intractable four branch pattern. In this last, there is a division of executive officials. The "come and go" presidents concentrate upon their public images and selected headline issues while the "permanent" administrative forces perform much of the specialized policy making in the manner of a coordinate fourth branch.

That pattern of operations has disturbed many officials and professional observers of the government for several decades and there have been repeated efforts to get the four-branch-practice back into the bottle of three-branch-theory. But political science analysts continue to report persistent presidential-administrative separation in the executive system. A new approach may be in order. We may ask whether four branch government is really outside the fundamentals of the Constitution. If the recurring division of decision making between presidential and bureaucratic realms does serve the goals of constitutional distribution, then direct influence upon specialized administrators may be legitimate as well as pragmatic and "democratic" responsibilities may include "public" participation in the processes which seek to guide particular officials directly as well as in the processes which involve the presidency.

The four branch model may not be descriptive of the government in all situations but the probability that it is appropriate at least as often as the three branch pattern makes consideration of it helpful or even essential to a full understanding of the operation of the government and of the means of endeavoring to control the administrative decisions.

This book seeks to aid reappraisal of the problem by examining the principles of constitutional distribution as a basis for ascertaining whether government by four coordinate branches—congressional, presidential, judicial and administrative—is constitutionally functional or dysfunctional.

The inquiry is pertinent because political science descriptions of the government often declare with respect to the Constitution the doctrine of separate powers among Congress, the president and the courts and then, in explaining operations, assert that there is a persistent division of policy making between the White House presidential realm and the career administrative forces.[1] Several leading analysts apply the term "fourth

1

branch of government" in explaining separations within the executive complex,[2] without saying definitely whether this is constitutionally functional or not. The reports of four branch operation seem to assume an enduring combination of underlying causes, including the emphasis of presidents upon their public relations roles, their ready use of White House assistants and advisers, the complexity of governmental activities and departmental arrangements, the influence of congressional subcommittees and the courts upon executive decisions, and the career orientation of most of the civil service in contrast to the short tenure of the presidential executive forces. A foremost analyst says that the "constitutional picture is far from clear regarding control over the administrative branch"[3] and another asserts that "the Constitution is a fallible and incomplete guide to national policy-making. Instead of three branches of government, each with its clearly defined sphere of competence and activity," he suggests that "there may be five branches of government in any particular issue area, or seven, or twenty, or only one."[4]

The main chapters of the book, which relate to separate, mixed and specialized arrangements of governmental authority, examine the explicit and implicit principles of constitutional distribution with the objective of ascertaining their purposes, methods and dimensions. But first, the short initial chapter reviews the unsystematic recognition by political scientists of the working separation within the formal executive branch. We will see that a division of officials cuts across institutional categories. The differentiating terms include noncareer and career, political and professional, and presidential and permanent, with no set entirely satisfactory. The boundary is not rigid even in fact. The autonomy of an administrative official may vary with his anonymity. The presidential executive force reaches out for headline issues and usually it can corral them. As a consequence, the independence of an operating unit or official from White House pressures often may depend upon staying out of the headlines, at least the front page Washington ones.

This touches upon a more popular basis of differentiation. Presidents are highly visible and newsworthy whereas specialized administrators usually are not. The mass media and much of the public tend to assume that the president, the members of Congress and the judges of the Supreme Court are our only policy makers. Yet those officials are merely the tip of the policy making iceberg. Most of that iceberg consists of the continuing officials of the administrative bureaucracy. We cannot be sure how definitely the visible and invisible portions are connected or which is really the cause of inaction or action in many particular situations. But we can be sure that the administrative bureaucracy is vast and multifariously pervasive. A president may help to identify the headline issues but necessarily the number of such matters is limited and what presidents leave to the administrative forces much exceeds in number and even in total impact what they take over for the White House. As we will see, the general picture presented by the political scientists who undertake to explain the general operation of the government is that presidential control actually extends only to selected matters and not to the regular actions of many executive officials, particularly the thousands of career administrators who seem to run most of the offices and bureaus most of the time.

In brief, neither the three power model nor the four branch one, with the presidency and the bureaucracy in coordinate positions, is fully or continuously descriptive of the American national government but the four branch pattern reflects the reality at least as often or as much as the three branch one. Thus, it seems educationally relevant or even necessary to consider whether the separate presidential and administrative forces are constitutionally functional as coordinate branches along with the congressional and judicial ones. To that end, the main purpose of this book is to analyze the pertinent principles of constitutional distribution.

The book explains that there are three distinguishable but often intermingled principles of governmental arrangement. The presentation identifies them with designations more specific than "separation of powers." The pattern of legislative, executive and judicial powers vested separately in Congress, the presidency and the courts, is termed "three-branch-separate-function government." The analysis of this principle of arrangement searches historical and legal data for light on such matters as the importance of the number of separate institutions and the necessity of a one-to-one correspondence between types of functions and the set of separated institutions.

The principle of arrangement in the main body of the Constitution is designated "mixed power government." It embraces checks and balances and shared functions and it is derived in part from those constitutional prescriptions which give one or both houses of Congress and the presidency interdependent roles with respect to statutes, treaties, appointments, expenditures, execution of powers and other matters.

The third principle of authority distribution is designated "specialized government." It relates to departments, committees, and other agencies, and its constitutional basis is primarily in the provision authorizing Congress to enact laws "necessary and proper for carrying into execution" the powers vested in the government or in "any department or officer thereof."

We will examine separately the development and the character of each of these principles of governmental arrangement in order to ascertain how far the concept of four coordinate branches is compatible with the constitutional tenets of authority distribution.

NOTES

1. See Appendix A. Some explanations give a single general function, such as "making policy" a higher place than legislation, execution, adjudication or administration.

2. For identity of explanations using the "fourth branch" designation, see _infra_ Unsystematic Recognition of Presidential-Administrative Separation, fns. 43-61. This book concerns governmental branches, not outside ones, such as the press; see Douglass Cater The Fourth Branch of Government Boston: Houghton Mifflin (1959) and Charles Peters and James Fallows (Eds.) The System: The Five Branches of American Government New York: Praeger (1976). This last adds interest groups and the press to the three traditional branches.

3. Peter Woll Public Policy Cambridge, Mass.: Winthrop (1974) 235. In 1963 Professor Woll wrote that American bureaucracy is "not properly subject to complete control by Congress, the President, or the judiciary" and that it "functions within a checks-and-balances system in much the same way as the original three branches of government." Peter Woll American Bureaucracy W. W. Norton (1963) 174. Second Edition (1977) 248.

4. Nelson W. Polsby Congress and the Presidency Third Edition Englewood Cliffs, N.J.: Prentice-Hall (1976) 4.

UNSYSTEMATIC RECOGNITION
OF PRESIDENTIAL-ADMINISTRATIVE SEPARATION

The most obvious reason for the division of executive officials is that much of the time the White House and the career bureaucracy do not need each other.[1] A president can defuse public anxieties more adroitly with the aid of the Executive Office inner circle, while specialized administrators can find more constant support from congressional subcommittees. But there is a larger story behind that key fact.

The Supreme Court in 1867, while refusing to enjoin an "executive and political" duty "imposed on the President," said that "the President is the executive department."[2] Here we are concerned with relationships inside the executive branch. They have grown complex and divisive. Now political science analysts start with the idea "that the President and the Executive Branch are not synonymous."[3] The recognition of internal division is common even though unsystematic.[4] It may refer to civil service detachment more than to White House autonomy but it appears even in scholarly books on the presidency. Rowland Egger puts it this way: "Students of government and public affairs have for a long time pointed out that the bureaucracy has a life of its own quite separate from that of the Presidency as well as that of the other parts of the government." Grant McConnell asserts that the executive branch "is so divided and fragmented and its parts are often so autonomous that the president's power of command over them is often little more than a fiction." Philippa Strum observes that "the bureaucracy is a great jousting-place for challenges from the warriors of many competing camps" and that, in this arena, "the president is merely one competitor among many and history shows that he is far from the strongest."[5]

Other political scientists point out the responsiveness of the administrative officials to congressional units. Stephen K. Bailey states in his book on Congress: "The executive branch is not a neat pyramid of organization with the President at the top. It is a highly decentralized operation with a number of semiautonomous parts, and with most of its decisions ambiguously accountable both to the President and to parts of the Congress." Charles M. Hardin, in an analysis of presidential power, asserts that the bureaucracies "play the president off against Congress" and that in "their frustration, Congress and the president struggle against each other for the control of the bureaucracy--and therefore of policy; but bureaucracy escapes." Another specialist on the presidency, Dorothy B. James, explains that the "bureaucracy cannot be controlled by the President, Congress or any of the extra-constitutional actors involved" and that therefore "alliances have to be worked out."[6]

These statements indicate that the administrative realm is neither monolithic nor isolated. But all the branches are complex, interdependent structures, partly dependent upon and partly independent of each other. They are conglomerates with diverse relationships at various levels. We will see that there are countless interactions between bureaucratic and congressional subunits. In fact, those relationships give the administrative branch much of the continuing multiplicity of power which distinguishes it from the presidential executive branch and the alternating partisanism of the White House.[7]

The political science recognition of presidential-administrative separation varies considerably, and we will review the unsystematic expressions of it under three headings: the division of executive officials, the centricity of administrative units, and the permanence of the executive division.

The Division of Executive Officials

Key political science analyses of presidential-administrative relationships emphasize the differences between noncareer and career appointees. "The Civil Service Act created a dichotomy within the executive branch between career and noncareer administrators" which "has become an immutable and an *essential* feature of our fragmented executive structure," Louis C. Gawthrop asserts in his analysis of administrative politics.[8] The noncareer executives appointed by the presidents usually serve for less than four years[9] and reflect the alternating partisanism of the White House. In contrast, top Civil Service administrators are apt to have experience records of twenty years or more and to be much less partisan in their policy decisions.

The boundary between the "political" executives of the presidential branch and the "permanent" officials of the administrative branch is less a line than a zone. Moreover, it may vary with the place and the time. In general, it cuts horizontally across the three categories of official institutions, that is, the Executive Office of the President, the Executive Departments and the Independent Agencies. Each category, of course, has both noncareer and career officials. The boundary zone includes officials who are not clearly or consistently either presidential or permanent in status. Those in such an "undistributed middle" may be some but not all of the executives in four sub-levels, that is, (1) the outer cabinet, usually the heads of the departments other than State, Defense, Treasury and Justice;[10] (2) the presidential appointees in the Independent Agencies; (3) the "political" bureau administrators and assistant secretaries in the departments; and (4) those "supergrade" civil servants with other than career assignments.

Accordingly, the presidential executive branch consists, primarily but not entirely, of the White House staff, the top officials of the Executive Office of the President, and the inner cabinet.

Recognition of this division of the formal executive branch seems essential to a proper understanding of the presidency because that office invariably has lesser degrees of influence over the lower levels and the outer reaches of the executive universe. [11]

The existing presidential-administrative separation involves not only the division of executive officials into two general classes but also a mixed distribution of functions within the government. Many professionals engage in specialized legislative and adjudicative functions as well as executive ones. Peter Woll, a leading analyst of the national administration, asserts that the bureaucracy developed "to fill the gap created by the inability of the other branches" to meet all the requirements of modern government. He explains that the policy process is highly fragmented because its scope and complexity require "functional specialization and a division of labor." This is "reflected in congressional committees, and even more importantly, in the bureaucracy." As a result, "administrative agencies are the focal points of governmental policy-making." He also observes that "administrative *functions* are not so much executive as they are *legislative* and *judicial*." Insofar as they are legislative, "it is natural for Congress to consider the agencies as an extension of itself;" insofar as they are judicial "Congress feels in many instances that administrative independence is desirable." [12] For these reasons administrators are apt to be at least as responsive to congressional committees and courts as to the higher executive officials. [13]

The extent to which specialized administrative units are operationally separate from the White House does not seem to have a necessary connection to their official organizational category. The units which have been at times sharply in conflict with presidential forces include the Central Intelligence Agency, the Federal Bureau of Investigation and the Federal Reserve Board. The first is supervised by the National Security Council in the Executive Office of the President, the second is in a cabinet department (Justice) and the third is an Independent Agency. [14]

There is wide recognition that non-departmental regulatory agencies, such as the Federal Trade Commission, the National Labor Relations Board and the Interstate Commerce Commission are really as much legislative and judicial as executive. For one thing, their regulatory orders may be reviewed directly by the Courts of Appeals. However, there are many departmental agencies of a similar character, such as those dealing with commodity exchange (Agriculture), navigable waters (Army), education and food and drugs (Health, Education and Welfare), wages and hours (Labor) and aviation administration (Transportation). Also, there are other departmental units which engage extensively in specialized legislation and adjudication, such as those relating to patents and trademarks (Commerce), Indian affairs (Interior), immigration and naturalization (Justice) and internal revenue and customs (Treasury). The new Department of Energy embodies a regulatory board with quasi-legislative and quasi-judicial powers.

Many agencies within the departments are noted for their high degree of independence from the White House and for their responsiveness to Congress. "The plain truth is that such powerful subordinate organizations as the Bureau of Public Roads, Army Corps of Engineers, Public Health Service, National Park Service, and Forest Service constitute the departmental power centers and are quite capable of making it on their own without Secretarial help, except when challenged by strong hostile, external forces," Harold Seidman wrote after many years in the Bureau of the Budget. "Often," he observed, "they can do more for the Secretary than he can do for them." [15]

The idea that sub-departmental units form autonomous parts of a coordinate administrative branch may run counter to a belief that the cabinet provides a command link between the presidency and the operating units. However, several political scientists, who have given the matter special thought, maintain that the cabinet occupies an ambivalent position in both policy formation and managerial direction. There are differences among cabinet members, of course, but each is substantially in an intermediate position, responsive to the constituent bureaus of the respective department as well as to the White House. An inner cabinet member who participates in presidential policy-making is most likely to act in a special role and to serve more as a staff adviser than as an administrator. [16] But even inner cabinet members face the conflict between presidential and departmental forces. Thomas E. Cronin, in his survey of interviews with White House staff members and departmental officials, explains the general conflict as well as the added estrangement of the outer cabinet. "Every White House has problems with the departments and agencies," he asserts, and he refers to the "troubled relations between the White House staff and the executive departments as a factor in constraining the president's ability to implement policy." [17]

Several other political scientists point out the divided role of the department heads. Erwin C. Hargrove notes that the "cabinet officers face two ways, upward to the President and Presidential government and downward to the permanent government" and that "the President cannot rely upon the department heads he has appointed to serve his point of view completely." [18] Louis C. Gawthrop explains the effects upon the theory of hierarchical command. "In short, the President has limited control of his Cabinet and sub-Cabinet members; they in turn have limited control over the operations of their own subordinates." [19] Aaron Wildavsky asserts that the department heads "must serve more than one master." They are "necessarily beholden to Congress for appropriations and for substantive legislation," and they "are expected to speak for the major interests entrusted to their care, as well as for the President." This means, he adds, that the department heads "need cooperation from the bureaucracy" to gain the support of the special interests. [20] Robert C. Fried states that quite often "the political executives nominally heading the departments" become "captive" advocates for the constituent bureaus. [21] William E. Mullen also makes this point. "If cabinet secretaries are to assure full working cooperation with the permanent members of the bureaucracy, they must come to identify with the goals and standards of those

8

professionals and seek to protect their interests." As a consequence, he adds, those in the White House come to feel that the department head is "being controlled by the department, rather than controlling it for the president." He explains the basic conflict. "The more they speak for the agency and its clients, the less they speak for the chief executive."[22] Richard F. Fenno, Jr., probably the foremost analyst of cabinet behavior, summarizes the situation. He states that "the realities of the Cabinet member's existence are not alone his dependent, contingent, hierarchical relationship to the President, but his independent, self-regulating, polyarchical relationships to non-presidential centers of power."[23]

The difficulties which presidents encountered in striving for unified command of the executive branch led to the establishment in 1939 of the Executive Office of the President. Its main units have been the White House staff, the Bureau of the Budget, now the principal portion of the Office of Management and Budget, the Council of Economic Advisers (1946) and the National Security Council (1947). The various staffs have increased in total many times over.[24] In recent years, presidents have promised to reduce the size of at least the White House staff but the Executive Office-White House contingent is still overwhelming.[25] In fact, it is a bureaucratic department in itself.[26] Yet it has not resulted in greater control by the White House. "A full generation's experience with bigger and better presidencies has left the situation substantially unchanged," observes Robert C. Wood, a political scientist with cabinet experience.[27] Frederick C. Thayer asserts that the "persistent drive for overhead consolidation may be marching us to the rear."[28] Executive relationships may vary somewhat from time to time.[29] The Jimmy Carter White House promptly urged managerial autonomy among departmental officials and then concentrated upon a publicized stream of symbolic impressions, counteracting images or anxieties, and crisis-elevated legislative proposals.[30]

The Centricity of Administrative Units

Political science explanations of governmental operations base presidential-administrative separation not only upon the mixed situation of the cabinet members, but also upon the central role of the constituent units of the departments. Grant McConnell says that "the bureaus and agencies of the federal government often have their own political sources of support and can act independently of presidential wishes." Louis W. Koenig explains that the "single most powerful figure in the great pyramid is the bureau chief, who in many subtle ways can frustrate the President's purposes when they diverge from his own."[31] Harold Seidman sets forth sharply the central, dominant position of the bureau administrators. "It is the agency heads, not the President, who have the men, money, materiel, and legal powers."[32] Richard E. Neustadt declares that while agency administrators are responsible to the president, "they *also* are responsible to Congress, to their clients, to their staffs, and to themselves." In short, he concludes, "they have five masters."[33] That finding accords with

Professor Neustadt's contention that the power of the presidency is not to command but to persuade.[34] Philippa Strum points out that "the real power in each bureaucracy lies with the middle-level management: those civil servants who make the day-to-day decisions and keep the bureaucracy functioning in spite of the vagaries of electoral politics." Dorothy James observes: "Civil service employees have become a separate group organized to bargain effectively with all other elements in the political system." [35]

Other political scientists also stress the centricity of subdepartmental units. James MacGregor Burns speaks of "the organizational outer limits of dependable presidential influence" and observes that bureau heads "operate nominally under presidential direction but actually in response to many other influences." He explains that "typically a bureau holds a position of quasi independence from President, Congress, clientele group, and public, and of quasi dependence on them" so that "as best he can the agency chief works out his own 'mix' of organizational alliances and independencies." [36] Hugh Heclo asserts: "The administrative machinery in Washington represents a number of fragmented power centers rather than a set of subordinate units under the President." Morton H. Halperin stresses the continuity of the professional specialists. "All Presidents are dependent on the permanent bureaucracies of government inherited from their predecessors," he declares, adding that the president's "limited freedom to maneuver" is "acute in all areas" but that the military "poses a unique set of problems for him."[37] Theodore Lowi points out that the "most formidable barrier" to central control "is not size or complexity but *integrity*—the integrity of the separate bureaus, the integrity of professional specialities, and the integrity of careers that begin with advanced training and end in a lifetime of dedication to a particular problem of conquest."[38] One of the related causes of executive branch division is the persistent tendency of presidents to concentrate upon selected issues. David B. Truman noted this in his 1951 landmark volume: "The president's necessary detachment from numerous issues of administrative policy inevitably imposes a large measure of independence upon department heads, whether or not they are personally attached to his policies."[39] A 1977 analysis makes a similar point: "Professional bureaucrats dominate those vast segments of the policy process that do not become major issues."[40]

Rowland Egger, in his descriptive analysis of the president of the United States, sets forth a number of reasons that the president and the bureaucracy "find themselves attempting to move in different directions:"[41]

The first of these derives from the simplistic fact that the bureaucracy is permenent and the President is temporary. The second is that in our special sort of bureaucratic system the bureaucrat is not only permanent in tenure but permanent in place, that is, that careers are not in the civil service, but in the Internal Revenue Service or the Bureau of the Mines. The third is that the loyalties of bureaucrats in the United States

10

government are program loyalties, not loyalties to the service or to the government and certainly not to the President. The fourth is that the more familiar and congenial relationships of the top bureaucracy are with congressional committee and subcommittee chairmen and with lobbyists and interest-group leaders, not with the Office of Management and Budget or with the paratrooping presidential aides from the White House Office.

This last assumes what other political scientists have said, that is, that career administrators often are more responsive to congressional units than to presidential appointees in the executive branch.[42]

Several scholarly analysts during the past quarter century have declared that the United States government now has separate presidential and administrative branches. Ernest S. Griffith in his 1951 study of Congress, asserted that "a strong case can be made out that we actually have 'four-way' government instead of the classic tripartite" and the "Congress, the presidency, the bureaucracy, and the judiciary are the four."[43] Norton Long, in a 1952 article "Bureaucracy and Constitutionalism" concluded: "The theory of our constitution needs to recognize and understand the working and the potential of our great fourth branch of government, taking a rightful place beside President, Congress and Courts."[44] Then in 1963, Peter Woll's volume on the national bureaucracy stated that "the administrative branch adds a fourth dimension to the constitutional system of separation of powers, a dimension which is not controlled within its framework." He concluded that "American bureaucracy takes its place as an equal partner with the President, Congress and the judiciary."[45] In 1965, the historian Arthur M. Schlesinger, Jr., in his account of John F. Kennedy's "thousand days" wrote that "with an activist President it became apparent that there was a fourth branch: the Presidency itself." That may suggest that the presidency is the cause of the separation.[46] Professor Koenig's 1968 edition of his work on chief executives reported that the Kennedy administration "in its private comment seemed to adopt the notion that the President must contend not merely with Congress but with a further branch, a fourth branch, the bureaucracy." Later, in a 1969 article, Professor Schlesinger said that there are "four branches" and he identified the separate character of a "presidential government" and a "permanent government."[47]

Political scientists have made increasing reference to a "fourth branch of government". James W. Davis, Jr., in a 1970 analysis of the national executive system explained that it "is possible to view the President and the Executive Branch as separate branches, with one or the other being the fourth branch," or to view them as components of one unit, like the two houses of Congress, but "the important point is that the President and the Executive Branch are not the same."[48] The houses of Congress are, of course, much like separate branches because they can check and balance each other; each may defeat bills adopted by the other. Such a relationship between the presidency and the administrative force is a new concept for most Americans. Dale Vinyard, in a 1971 book on the presidency pointed out that some persons apply the phrase "fourth branch of government" to the "thousands of civil servants" . . . . who in fact, do most of the executing of the laws." He also stated that all governmental agencies are subject to a variety of pressures and that there "is no guarantee that the president will have the greatest influence on a particular agency."[49] Charles E. Jacob's 1972 analysis of "The Presidential Institution" and "The Bureaucractic Appendage" was more specific:[50]

> While bureaucracy (or administration) is in many ways executive in nature—and thus commonly considered to be an offshoot of the presidency—both in terms of the diversity of its responsibilities and its tenuous relationship to the presidential office, it must be viewed as a fourth branch of government.

Then Emmet John Hughes, one time adviser to President Eisenhower, stated in his 1973 volume on the "living presidency" that "such are this bureaucracy's formidable size and independent disposition that it can loom as an almost autonomous fourth branch of the government." He gave several reasons for "the distance separating" the presidential office and the "federal bureaucracy." He also indicated that the use of the term "branch" is not to suggest complete homogeneity but rather disassociation from the presidency and certain other institutions.[51] Peter Woll and Rochelle Jones asserted in September 1973 that "the bureaucracy has become a fourth branch of government, separate and independent of the President, Congress and the courts."[52] Their April 1974 article declared that the "bureaucracy cannot and should not be controlled completely by the President, Congress or the courts."[53] William L. Morrow's book on public administration in 1975 stated that "agency independence has led to the accusation that the bureaucracy constitutes, in effect, a powerful fourth branch of government" and that agencies "choose their allies and then resist challenges to their programs."[54] He identified agencies within the departments of H E W, Interior, Agriculture, Army, Justice and Transportation.

Each of these observations seems to apply the term "fourth branch" broadly, that is, to embrace administrative policy makers in the departments as well as in the non-departmental agencies.[55]

The idea of a separate administrative branch appears to have penetrated to an appreciable degree the political science profession generally. We may test the extent of this development by examining the texts used in the basic university course in American national government. That course is a comprehensive vehicle, and the texts for it are about the only place that members of the discipline bring together the fruits of the various subdisciplines concerned with the American national system of government and politics. The course generally has the largest enrollment, and it is the only political science offering taken by many university students. Nearly all of the more than fifty-five basic texts expressly assert in some degree that the president regularly is not in full control of the executive branch.[56] More than thirty such volumes have separate chapters on the "administration" or "bureaucracy" apart from the chapters on the presidency. In several texts the chapters on the four types of

institutions--legislative, executive, judicial and administrative--are separate parts of a general subdivision with varying generic titles.[57]
Moreover, twelve of the volumes expressly employ the term "fourth
branch" in relation to the administrative officialdom.[58]

The several analysts who use the term "fourth branch" do not present
a common definition or characterization. But all seem to assume that it
includes the career administrators and the other civil service or merit
system appointees who engage in making policy. Whether it also includes
any presidential appointees is not always clear.

The foremost effort to identify and characterize the two branches of
the executive/administrative conglomeration seems to be that of Professor Schlesinger in his 1969 article:[59]

> The rise of modern bureaucracy has divided the executive
> branch between the presidential government and the permanent
> government. In this complex relationship, the presidential
> government has preferences and policies backed by a presumed
> mandate from the electorate. But the permanent government
> has preferences and policies of its own. It has vested interests of
> its own in programs; it has alliances of its own with congressional
> committees, lobbies, and the press; it has its own particular, and
> not seldom powerful, constituencies. Also, it is around longer.
> We now have, in consequence, four branches of government. An
> activist President may have quite as much trouble with the
> federal bureaucracy as with the legislative or judicial branches.

Professor Schlesinger's designations of "presidential" and "permanent" may
not provide an absolute, complete division of executive officials but they
do furnish a general basis for explaining the upper and lower levels of the
executive branch. The boundary is a zone more than a line, and it may be
a wide and fluctuating zone. A number of political scientists have found
these terms appropriate.[60] For instance, Erwin C. Hargrove, a specialist
on the presidency, undertakes to define the two terms in his 1974 volume
on the power of the modern presidency:[61]

> . . . The Presidential government is that thin layer of Presi-
> dential appointees in the White House and Presidential agencies
> and at the top of each department . . . . The permanent
> government is composed of all those civil servants whose jobs are
> secure regardless of changes of Administration.

There may be some officials who are neither "presidential" nor "permanent" but here we are concerned with the major division of the appointed
policy makers. The definitions seem to support our definition of the
administrative branch as the non-presidential portion of the executive
branch. They also support the idea that the career officials are the main
portion of the administrative branch.

13

The Permanence of the Executive Division

Published reports of presidential-administrative separation go back at least to Franklin Roosevelt's accounts of intractability at the Navy Department.[62] Presidents have sought to close the gaps through reorganizations[63] and more staff assistants and advisers.[64] However, such efforts toward full executive unity have been in general non-productive or even counter-productive.[65] Now, presidents more and more are meeting demands to be public relations personalities,[66] while the decisions of specialized administrators are increasingly the mainstream of governmental policy making despite the "ultimate" authority of the elected institutions.[67] Political scientists recognize this contrast of presidential few and bureaucratic many. Professor Vinyard explains that the president "must deal with those matters he considers most important or urgent or troublesome, leaving much of the bureaucracy free to operate at the discretion of its administrators."[68] Professor Polsby notes that a president can change a particular agency's policies "if he is willing to bear the costs in terms of time, energy" and other burdens but a president "is free to pursue those policies that are of greatest concern to him." Hence, he adds, we can expect "that most agencies most of the time will conduct their business according to the same pattern no matter who is President."[69] Control tends to depend, for the president as for Congress, upon specificity of direction, and presidents can be specific about only a comparatively few matters. Jimmy Carter was anxious to revise administrative procedures and to establish a different pattern of relationships among White House assistants and departmental officials. But by the end of 1977 there was much evidence that conditions and the force of circumstances made most such innovations impracticable. More and more the manner of operation settled into the procedures and methods characteristic of previous regimes.

Presidents, of course, have many things to consider other than relationships with career administrators. They must serve several masters--the diverse electoral publics, the socio-economic situation, the national security configuration and the diplomatic objectives as well as the traditional moral beliefs of the nation, the congressional leaders, and their own personal-political situation. Also, the roles of sovereign representative, commander in chief, symbolic personality, and legislative initiator are more important than that of chief administrator. "Presidential reputations," Professor Fried asserts, "are made in policy and political leadership, rather than in managing the executive branch."[70]

Basic operating differences between the presidency and the bureau administrators also contribute to the persistent chasm. The president is most often a generalist; the administrators are, of course, specialists. The one is highly newsworthy while generally the others are not. The route to the presidency is partisan politics; merit system appointments are meant to be non-political. The people expect presidents to personify ideals, hopes and goals while they assume--or maybe should assume--that civil servants exemplify technical proficiency, legal duty and fixed procedure. The one has a two four-year-term limitation and his closest advisers and assistants come and go at least as rapidly. The civil service administrators have a career opportunity and many are veterans of twenty years service or more. They are protected from patronage or general policy removal and take pride in continuing neutrality from the alternating partisanism of the White House.

The tendency of the White House and the specialized administrators to operate separately of each other reflects, most basically, the contrast between the presidential tenure and the career status of the merit system appointees. No president, by reorganization or otherwise, can or will change that situation to any appreciable degree. Nor will Congress do so. The career opportunity for the civil service and other merit systems will remain. Moreover, the large ratio of career administrators to noncareer ones--now ten to one[71]--is most likely to continue. Short tenure for presidents and hence for their closest advisers, is even more a fixture Presidents serve an average of about six years; recently it has been four years. Eight years is the general limit and a president must spend the first two years learning the "ropes" and the last two being a "lame duck." [72] A single six year term would be no improvement in this regard.[73] Accordingly, the difference in tenure is sufficient in itself to assure the continuing division within the formal executive branch.

Other causal conditions for the separation also are strong and pervasive. They include the multifarious intricacy of our socio-economic system, the extensive governmental involvement in development, regulation and protection of that system,[74] and the application of "the rule of law" to the massive, complex governmental operations.[75] The amount of legislative and adjudicative action undertaken by administrative officials means that they are as relevant to the congressional and judicial branches as to the presidential executive one. Likewise, the extent to which the administrative officialdom has specialized expertise and experience makes it at least as essential to modern government as the other three branches.[76]

The separation within the executive system derives from developments with respect to the presidency as well as those relating to the administrative bureaucracy. A veteran newspaper commentator describes the essence of such changes. "Beginning with Kennedy the president became progressively less a man who presided over the processes of government in Washington and became progressively more a one-man generator and executor of national policy." [77] The standing of a president may benefit more from reform proposals conceived to relieve public anxieties than from the execution of laws. Legislation is often a delayed bundle of compromises and application is apt to entail irritating regulations and impersonal actions. That is indicated in a statement by a former White House adviser to Professor Cronin: "It is more important to symbolize solutions than it is to achieve them in operations. Getting legislation passed or getting a department to do things "is never" as important as talking to the people through the media and providing symbolic leadership about new directions." [78] The permanence of the

15

presidential emphasis upon external imagery is attested by the prominence of each new White House staff in the public policy activity of the successive presidents.[79]

NOTES

1. "By law, the President of the United States is Chief of the Executive Branch, but in fact he can be ignored and frustrated by employees and organizations that do not need him and will continue long after he has gone." James W. Davis, Jr., The National Executive Branch New York: Free Press (1970) 1. " . . . the careerists who ultimately must implement presidential policy no longer have as much of a stake in its success. They need only wait long enough and there will be another President." Stephen Hess Organizing the Presidency Washington: The Brookings Institution (1976) 153. "A President, these days, is an invaluable clerk. His services are in demand all over Washington. His influence, however, is a very different matter. Laws and customs tell us little about leadership in fact." Richard E. Neustadt Presidential Power: The Politics of Leadership New York: Wiley (1976) 74. See fns. 42, 68, 69, and 79 infra.

2. Mississippi v. Johnson 4 Wall. (71 U.S.) 475, 500 (1867). The Supreme Court denied Mississippi's request for an injunction restraining President Andrew Johnson from enforcing the Reconstruction Acts.

3. Davis op. cit. 1.

4. See Appendix A. " . . . most of the administrative agencies are placed in the executive branch. But their accountability to the chief executive and their subjection to his exclusive direction and control do not automatically follow from the mere fact that they are elements of the executive establishment." ' Joseph E. Kallenbach The American Chief Executive: The Presidency and the Governorship New York: Harper and Row (1966) 377.

5. Rowland Egger The President of the United States Second Edition New York: McGraw-Hill (1972) 44; Grant McConnell The Modern Presidency Second Edition New York: St. Martin's (1976) 61; Philippa Strum Presidential Power and American Democracy Pacific Palisades, Calif.: Goodyear (1972) 41.

6. Stephen K. Bailey Congress in the Seventies New York: St. Martin's (1970) 27; Charles M. Hardin Presidential Power and Accountability: Toward a New Constitution Chicago: University of Chicago Press (1974) 15; and Dorothy B. James The Contemporary Presidency Second Edition Indianapolis: Bobbs-Merrill (1974) 212.

7. See infra The Legitimacy of Specialized Government--Specialized Control of Administrative Functions.

8. Louis C. Gawthrop Administrative Politics and Social Change New York: St. Martin's (1971) 24, 25. On merit systems generally, see David Rosenbloom Federal Service and the Constitution Ithaca, N.Y.: Cornell University Press (1971) 11.

9. David Stanley, Dean E. Mann and Jameson W. Doig **Men Who Govern: A Biographical Profile of Federal Political Executives** Washington: The Brookings Institution (1967) 55-68; Dean E. Mann and Jameson W. Doig **The Assistant Secretaries: Problems and Processes of Appointment** Washington: The Brookings Institution (1965) 227-31. Hugh Heclo **A Government of Strangers: Executive Politics in Washington** Washington: The Brookings Institution (1977) 1-3; 101-102; 103-109.

10. On the differentiation of the inner and outer cabinets, see Thomas E. Cronin **The State of the Presidency** Boston: Little, Brown (1975) 188-201; Harold Seidman **Politics, Position and Power: The Dynamics of Federal Organization** New York: Oxford University Press (1970) 100-101; Erwin C. Hargrove **The Power of the Modern Presidency** Philadelphia: Temple University Press (1974) 238-39.

11. For illustration, we may identify six levels of policy making discretion—Presidential, Secretarial, Assistant Secretarial, Administrator-Director, Civil Service Supergrade, and Regular Civil Service. Quite roughly, there are from 50 to 100 policy forming officials in the first two levels, 500 to 1,000 in the middle two, and 5,000 to 10,000 in the lower two levels.

12. Peter Woll **American Bureaucracy** New York: Norton (1977) 248; **Public Policy** Cambridge, Mass.: Winthrop (1974) 15, 29; **American Bureaucracy** 63 "As the scale and complexity of government increased, civil servants assumed a larger role in policy-making . . . . administrators assumed discretionary powers that tended in a simpler era to remain in the hands of elected representatives." Robert Presthus **Public Administration** Sixth Edition New York: Ronald Press (1975) 1.

13. Robert C. Fried **Performance in American Bureaucracy** Boston: Little Brown (1976) 232, 233, 261; William L. Morrow **Public Administration: Politics and the Political System** New York: Random House (1975) 113-14; See also fn. 42 **infra.**

14. On the general character of the types of Independent Agencies, see Seidman **op. cit.** 215-35; Davis **op. cit.** 33-42; Fried **op. cit.** 378-79; Cronin **op. cit.** 189 and Lewis C. Mainzer **Political Bureacracy** Glenview, Ill.: Scott, Foresman (1973) 22.

15. Seidman **op. cit.** 100; see also **Ibid.** 127, 132; Fried **op. cit.** 111, 112; and Presthus **op. cit.** 378.

16. Seidman **op. cit.** 100-101.

17. Cronin **op. cit.** 154, 155-210.

18. Hargrove **op. cit.** 238.

19. Gawthrop **op. cit.** 24.

20. Aaron Wildavsky "The Past and Future Presidency" 41 **The Public Interest** (Fall, 1975) 67.

21. Fried **op. cit.** 207. See also James MacGregor Burns **Presidential Government: The Crucible of Leadership** Sentry Edition Boston: Houghton Mifflin (1973) 129-30.

22. William E. Mullen **Presidential Power and Politics** New York: St. Martin's Press (1976) 189.

23. Richard F. Fenno, Jr., "Presidential-Cabinet Relations: A Pattern and a Case Study" 52 **American Political Science Review** (March 1958) 388-405 at 391; David E. Haight and Larry D. Johnston (Eds.) **The President: Roles and Powers** Chicago: Rand McNally (1965) 214.

24. Cronin op. cit. 118-51.

25. Louis W. Koenig The Chief Executive Third Edition New York: Harcourt Brace Jovanovich (1975) 11; The New York Times March 31, 1977 A 20.

26. "The Brownlow Report of 1937 and its sequel 'The Executive Office of the President' established not alone an organization, but a doctrine: the rightness of a 'President's Department,' the need for staff resources of his own." Richard E. Neustadt "Politicians and Bureaucrats," David B. Truman (Ed.) The Congress and America's Future Second Edition Englewood Cliffs, N.J.: Prentice-Hall (1973) 118-40 at 130.

27. Robert C. Wood "When Government Works" Aaron Wildavsky (Ed.) Perspectives on the Presidency Boston: Little, Brown (1975) 393-404 at 396. See also C. Herman Pritchett "The President's Constitutional Position" Thomas E. Cronin and Rexford G. Tugwell (Eds.) The Presidency Reappraised Second Edition New York: Praeger (1977) 3-23 at 19; Cronin op. cit. (fn 10) 138 and Koenig op. cit. 185.

28. Frederick C. Thayer "Presidential Policy Processes and 'New Administration': A Search for Revised Paradigms" Stanley Bach and George T. Sulzner (Eds). Perspectives on the Presidency Lexington, Mass.: D.C. Heath (1974) 267-81 at 268.

29. Robert S. Gilmour "The Institutionalized Presidency: A Conceptual Clarification" Norman C. Thomas (Ed.) The Presidency in Contemporary Context New York: Dodd, Mead (1975) 147-59 at 158-59.

30. The New York Times Dec. 1, 1976; Jan. 21-25, 1977; Apr. 16-21, 1977; May 12, 1977; May 22, 1977, 1, E3.

31. McConnell op. cit. 75; Koenig op. cit. 184.

32. Seidman op. cit. 73.

33. Richard E. Neustadt Presidential Power: The Politics of Leadership New York: John Wiley & Sons (1976) 107; (1960 Ed. 39).

34. Ibid. 101-25; (1960 Ed. 33-57)

35. Strum op. cit. 42; James op. cit. 205.

36. Burns op. cit. 140, 141.

37. Hugh Heclo A Government of Strangers: Executive Politics in Washington Washington: The Brookings Institution (1977) 12. Morton H. Halperin "The President and the Military" Wildavsky op. cit. (fn. 27) 487-99 at 487.

38. Theodore J. Lowi American Government: Incomplete Conquest Hinsdale, Ill.: Dryden Press (1976) 492.

39. David B. Truman The Governmental Process: Political Interests and Public Opinion New York: Alfred A. Knopf (1951) 408; reprinted in part "Presidential Executives or Congressional Executives?" Aaron Wildavsky (Ed.) The Presidency Boston: Little Brown (1969) 486-91 at 489.

40. Eugene Lewis American Politics in a Bureaucratic Age: Citizens Constituents, Clients and Victims Cambridge, Mass.: Winthrop (1977) 163.

41. Egger op. cit. (fn. 5) 45.

42. " . . . to say that it is the constitutional responsibility of the President to control the administrative branch is not accurate, because he was not given the tools to do so. Considering many agencies as arms of Congress is as much in accord with the Constitution as maintaining that

the bureaucracy is the responsibility of the President." Peter Woll American Bureaucracy New York: W. W. Norton (1977) 64; " . . . the president's direction of the executive branch is, in a sense, shared with the legislative branch and this is probably inevitable." Dale Vinyard The Presidency New York: Charles Scribner's Sons (1971) 117; " . . . the major check on presidential power may well be, not the Congress in its legislative capacity, but the Congress in its executive capacity allied with the bureaucracy and special interest groups." Strum op. cit. 46; "Congress, even when it is dominated by the president's party, often does not want to increase presidential discretion within executive agencies." Cronin op. cit. 69; another political scientist speaks of "the reluctance of Congress to give department heads effective control over their bureau chiefs." Ernest S. Griffith Congress: Its Contemporary Role New York: New York University Press (1951) 38. This matter is discussed infra. See The Wide Scope of Mixed Power Government (The Shared Control of Administration) and The Legitimacy of Specialized Government.

43. Griffith op. cit. 39.

44. Norton Long "Bureaucracy and Constitutionalism" 46 American Political Science Review (Sept. 1952) 808-18 at 818.

45. Peter Woll American Bureaucracy New York: Norton (1963) 25, 177; Second Edition (1977) 31, 252.

46. Arthur M. Schlesinger, Jr., A Thousand Days: John F. Kennedy in the White House Boston: Houghton Mifflin (1965) 680. Other have applied "fourth branch" to the presidency. "Some observers have characterized" the Executive Office of the President "as a fourth branch of government—a 'Presidential government' that stands apart from the 'permanent government' of the departments, agencies, and civil service." Hargrove op. cit. 79. Also, Philip B. Kurland Wall Street Journal, Dec. 12, 1973.

47. Koenig op. cit. (1968) 159. Arthur M. Schlesinger, Jr., "The Limits and Excesses of Presidential Power" Saturday Review May 3, 1969; reprinted as "Strengthening and Restraining the President" Robert S. Hirschfield (Ed.) The Power of the Presidency: Concepts and Controversy Second Edition Chicago: Aldine (1973) 364-72 at 368.

48. Davis op. cit. (fn. 1) 124.

49. Vinyard op. cit. (fn. 42) 116, 117.

50. Charles E. Jacob "The Presidential Institution" Gerald W. Pomper (Ed.) The Performance of American Government: Checks and Minuses New York: Free Press (1972) 236-57 at 252-53.

51. Emmet John Hughes The Living Presidency New York: Coward, McCann and Geoghegan (1973) 184, 185. "These reasons do not indict either the Presidential office as presumptuous or the 'fourth branch' as insubordinate. They simply explain the distance separating the two—under an overcast of mutual suspicion scarcely possible to break through." Ibid. 185.

52. Peter Woll and Rochelle Jones "Bureaucratic Defense in Depth" The Nation Sept. 17, 1973; reprinted David C. Saffell (Ed.) American Government: Reform in the Post-Watergate Era Cambridge, Mass.: Winthrop (1976) 181-87 at 182.

53. Peter Woll and Rochelle Jones "The Bureaucracy as a Check upon the Presidency" The Bureaucrat (April 1974) 8-20 at 19.

54. Morrow op. cit. (fn. 13) 102.

55. Some uses of "fourth branch" may have concerned only "independent agencies," such as the regulatory commissions; see Herman Miles Somers "The President as Administrator" David E. Haight and Larry D. Johnston (Eds.) The President: Roles and Powers Chicago: Rand, McNally (1965) 160-70 at 162; Charles E. Jacob "The Limits of Presidential Leadership" 62 South Atlantic Quarterly (Autumn 1963) 461-73, reprinted Sidney Warren (Ed.) The American President Englewood Cliffs, N.J.: Prentice-Hall (1967) 90-101 at 99.

56. See Appendix A.

57. The term 'policy making' enters the designation of such sections more than any other word or set of words. Other section titles use such designations as decision makers, public or political institutions, major branches, conversion structures, and political subsystems.

58. See Appendix A, items, 3, 6, 8, 20, 24, 33, 34, 38, 40, 48, 56 and 57. Also, item 1 includes the "bureaucracy" among "four legislative branches."

59. Schlesinger op. cit. (fn. 47 supra) 368.

60. See Appendix A, item 15.

61. Hargrove op. cit. (fn. 10) 238.

62. Burns op. cit. (fn. 21, supra) 142; John C. Livingston and Robert G. Thompson The Consent of the Governed Third Edition New York: MacMillan (1972) 401, 407. For Harry Truman's comment on the disillusionment that Dwight Eisenhower would have if he brought his military sense of command to the White House, see Neustadt op. cit. (fn. 33 supra) 77 (1960 ed. 9).

63. Presthus op. cit. (fn. 12, supra) 366-68; Gawthrop op. cit. (fn. 8, supra) 32-35; Richard P. Nathan "The President and the Bureaucracy in Domestic Affairs" Charles W. Dunn (Ed.). The Future of the American Presidency Morristown, N.J.: General Learning (1975) 118-26 at 122-23; Louis Fisher Presidential Spending Power Princeton, N.J.: Princeton University Press (1975) 40-58.

64. See "The Swelling of the Presidency" Cronin op. cit. (fn. 10, supra) 117-52; Presthus op. cit. (fn. 12, supra) 361-70.

65. "Every new administration gives fresh impetus to an age-old struggle between change and continuity, between political leadership and bureaucratic power. Bureaucrats have a legitimate interest in maintaining the integrity of government programs and organizations. Political executives are supposed to have a broader responsibility: to guide rather than merely reflect the sum of special interests at work in the executive branch.

"The search for effective political leadership in a bureaucracy of responsible career officials has become extraordinarily difficult in Washington. In every new crop of political appointees, some will have had government experience and a few will have worked together, but when it comes to group commitment to political leadership in the executive branch they constitute a government of strangers. And yet the fact remains that whether the President relies mainly on his White House aides or on his cabinet officials, someone is supposed to be mastering the bureaucracy 'out there.' For the President, his appointees, and high-ranking bureaucrats, the struggle to control the bureaucracy is usually a

leap into the dark." Hugh Heclo <u>A</u> <u>Government</u> <u>of</u> <u>Strangers:</u> <u>Executive</u>
<u>Politics</u> <u>in</u> <u>Washington</u> Washington: The Brookings Institution (1977) 1.
See also fn. 27, <u>supra</u>.

66. "The Presidency is the focus for the most intense and persistent
emotions in the American polity. The President is a symbolic leader, the
one figure who draws together the people's hopes and fears for the
political future." James David Barber <u>The</u> <u>Presidential</u> <u>Character:</u>
<u>Predicting</u> <u>Performance</u> <u>in</u> <u>the</u> <u>White</u> <u>House</u> Englewood Cliffs, N.J.
Prentice-Hall (1972) 4. See also Cronin <u>op.</u> <u>cit.</u> 34; Koenig <u>op.</u> <u>cit.</u> 11
and George E. Reedy <u>The</u> <u>Twilight</u> <u>of</u> <u>the</u> <u>Presidency</u> New York: New
American Library (1970) 21.

67. " . . . it is questionable whether the presidency has kept up with
the centrifugal tendency of the government." McConnell <u>op.</u> <u>cit.</u> 75.
See also Louis Fisher <u>President</u> <u>and</u> <u>Congress:</u> <u>Power</u> <u>and</u> <u>Policy</u> New
York: Free Press (1972) 82; fns. 31-37 <u>supra</u> and Appendix A, items 4,
13, 23, 31 and 56.

68. Vinyard <u>op.</u> <u>cit.</u> 116. See also fns. 39-41, <u>supra</u>.

69. Nelson W. Polsby <u>Congress</u> <u>and</u> <u>the</u> <u>Presidency</u> Third Edition
Englewood Cliffs, N.J.: Prentice-Hall (1976) 18.

70. Fried <u>op.</u> <u>cit.</u> 197.

71. One tabulation indicates a career-noncareer ratio of more than
fifteen to one. Presthus <u>op.</u> <u>cit.</u> 179.

72. Neustadt <u>op.</u> <u>cit.</u> (fn. 33 <u>supra</u>) 266-67.

73. "A president whose term was limited to one six-year stretch
would be a president who could command about two years of enthusiasm,
two years of acquiesence, and two years of obstruction." George E.
Reedy <u>The</u> <u>Twilight</u> <u>of</u> <u>the</u> <u>Presidency</u> New York: New American Library
(1970) 136.

74. See, in general, Murray Edelman <u>The</u> <u>Symbolic</u> <u>Uses</u> <u>of</u> <u>Politics</u>
Urbana, Ill.: University of Illinois Press (1964) 60-61.

75. "Under the principles of the separation of powers and the rule of
law, the courts are expected to keep administrative agencies from using
illegal, unfair, or unreasonable methods in achieving their goals." Fried
<u>op.</u> <u>cit.</u> 261.

76. " . . . the three primary branches have necessarily supported the
creation of a semiautonomous bureaucracy as an instrument to enable our
government to meet the challenges it has faced." Peter Woll <u>American</u>
<u>Bureaucracy</u> New York: Norton (1963) 174; Second Edition (1977) 248.
". . . It is easy to criticize the errors of omission and commission of
professional public bureaucracies, but it is even easier to see the problems
raised in a government administered by decentralized groups of amateurs.
Although there are problems, public bureaucracy seems able to maintain
an acceptable level of support from the citizenry. Barring a political
revolution, observers in the year 2000 will see public personnel systems
that are not too far different from what we have today. The forces that
will shape public personnel administration in the future are already
happening today. Affirmative action will force a sharpening of the tools
to measure merit; jobs will be restructured to accommodate upward
mobility from within; specialization and professionalization will continue.
The most active force in changing public personnel administration in the
future, however, will be the rise in power of public employee unions."

Fred A. Kramer _Dynamics of Public Bureaucracy_ Cambridge, Mass.: Winthrop (1977) 121.

77. Joseph C. Harsch _The Christian Science Monitor_ March 6, 1975.

78. Cronin _op. cit._ 10.

79. Stephen Hess, senior fellow at the Brookings Institution, identifies the characteristics of the "modern presidency." These include the "prodigious growth" of the Executive Office staffs and the "steadily rising influence of White House staff members as presidential advisers, with a corresponding decline in Cabinet influence." Likewise, there are "the President's increasing suspicion of the permanent government, leading to a vast proliferation of functional offices within the White House" and the expanding tendency of presidential assistants to be "special pleaders." Hess _op. cit._ 8, 9. Another political science study of the presidency concludes with this·sharp observation: "When people's attention.is focused solely on the man in the White House, they are misled into believing that they are witness to the essence of government. Actually they see only the drama and not the substance.   A democracy owes more to its citizens." Mullen _op. cit._ 265.

THE LIMITED SCOPE
OF SEPARATE FUNCTION GOVERNMENT

Whether the unsystematic but persistent separation of presidential and administrative forces in the operation of the United States government is constitutionally functional or dysfunctional involves the principles of authority distribution. Those principles are commonly, and somewhat roughly, known as "separation of powers" and "checks and balances." Their fundamental purposes are in general to prevent undue concentration of power and to assure the responsible exercise of authority. (In this subject area, "power" and "authority" often are used interchangeably.)

Analysts of the American system, including some Supreme Court justices, at times combine the principles of separate powers and of checks and balances under the name of one or the other, but this study will examine them as two distinct doctrines. The separate power principle is the most rigid as well as the most patent in constitutional presentation. It embodies the process of parallel vesting or the one-to-one correspondence of three types of functions and three institutions. We will designate it, at times, the three-branch-separate-function pattern of government. It is the structural facade of the Constitution. The initial clauses of Articles I, II, and III vest legislative, executive and judicial powers separately in a Congress, a president, and a Supreme Court. Those clauses were proposed halfway through the 1787 Convention, apparently to give the institutions more acceptable names than the terms "national legislature," "national executive," and "national judiciary," used in the proceedings to that point.[1]   The word "national" was anathema to many delegates, and it led to the mid-Convention switch to the term "United States." Supporters of ratification used "federal" apparently for similar reasons.   Yet the essential achievement of the Convention was to nationalize a major part of the internal sovereignty by authorizing Congress to regulate and tax individuals directly and by giving the national government the type of enforcement mechanism which the states had adopted in their constitutions of 1776-84, that is, separate institutions for execution and adjudication.   Six of the eleven new state constitutions had expressly declared the theory of separate powers or departments, and the 1789 constitution nationalized that pattern of distribution in giving the central government.substantial but limited authority over individuals within the states.

Whether the clause vesting "executive power" in a president furnishes any authority not specifically granted elsewhere has been debated repeatedly. The Virginia plan with which the 1787 Convention delegates began their deliberations proposed fairly general grants of legislative and executive "rights," but the delegations soon rejected that approach and

23

undertook to design specific authorizations. The legal bases of existing presidential power are particular constitutional grants, statutory enactments, and, in external and internal security matters, the inherent character of the office.

The national Constitution includes no explicit statement of the separate power doctrine, and those who favor such a principle tend to use the vesting clauses of the first three articles to serve many of its purposes. In one respect, those provisions go farther than the prior state declarations because the trio of vesting clauses suggests a one-to-one correspondence between a set of institutions and a set of functions. The simple rigidity of that pattern as well as the legal meaning possible for the term "powers" give the three clauses a transcendent potential when we enshrine them in our constitutional credo. But we may ask whether the establishment of three separate institutions was meant to be an end in itself or merely the start of a complex pattern of *functional* interrelationship. In our idealization of that elementary trio, we may overlook what the Founders considered to be the substance of the system, that is, the mixture of rights and duties and the interdependence of the various forces. During our two centuries of ideological history, the "separation of powers" may have stood at times for other allocation schemes or even for our whole system. That aided its reputation as "the most hallowed concept of constitutional theory and practice"[2] and as "the very character of the American political system."[3] But for the purposes of this critical inquiry, we need to consider what kind of force there is in the threefold design of the constitutional facade. In general, we will inquire whether it is a means to more basic objectives or is an end in itself. Particularly we need to know if it limits the number of coordinate branches despite the vast expansion of governmental authority and the increased complexity of operations.

This chapter will analyze, historically and legally, the pattern of three-branch-separate-function government, sketching its evolution, identifying its ideological essence, and reviewing the efforts of the Supreme Court to reconcile the doctrine of separate powers with the actual dispersion of types of functions among the congressional, presidential, judicial and administrative institutions.

The Evolution of the Separate Power Doctrine

The paradigm of separate legislative, executive and judicial powers was not history's first threefold pattern of government. The classical world had a theory of mixed sovereignty which combined the socio-political forces of the one, the few and the many, or, as Cicero said, monarchy, aristocracy and democracy. Modern adaptations have included the English Parliament of King, Lords and Commons and the colonial systems of governor, council and assembly. Most American constitutions embody a similar arrangement. For instance, a governor, senate and house of representatives form such a trio, and its essence is their mutual dependence in sharing the power to make superior policy.

The special essence of the doctrine of separate legislative, executive and judicial powers—in contrast to such theories as mixed representation, checks and balances or shared functions—is a combination of two beliefs. One is that government consists of legal, apolitical processes such as the enactment and application of penal statutes and adjudications under them. The other is that each process should be undertaken by a different institution so that a particular determination, such as criminal liability, is not concentrated in a single mortal or body of persons.

Political scientists and historians may differ on the exact origin of the separate process doctrine, but the three foremost scholars on the subject—Professors Francis D. Wormuth, William Gwyn, and M.J.C. Vile [4]—seem to agree that it emerged in the political and constitutional debates of the English civil war of the 1640s and 1650s. The particular occasion which brought forth the distinctive language of the separate function theory involved the efforts of the House of Commons to try its principal enemies—John Lilburne, the head of the Levelers and King Charles I—for criminal offenses.

The life of the doctrine at that time was primarily forensic, but the immediate objective throws light upon the force of "legislative" and "executive" as opposed to such terms as "parliament" and "king," or "democratic" and "monarchical," which had featured earlier maxims of mixed government or balanced constitution. The House of Commons, in judging persons on criminal charges, went beyond the impeachment procedure or the adoption of bills of attainder and undertook to hold trials either directly or through its appointed commissions. For instance, the House in 1645 called Lilburne before its Committee on Examinations for his refusal to take the Covenant oath, and it later had its Council of State imprison and interrogate him. Lilburne claimed that he was entitled to a hearing under settled rules of law rather than by arbitrary process and that the Commons had no law-executing power.[5] The assertion that Parliament had only legislative authority meant that it should not act as a trial court. On the basis of the debates at that time, Professor Wormuth identifies the origin of the separate power doctrine:[6]

> It seems, then, that the first purpose for which the separation of the legislative and executive powers was advocated was to insure that accused persons be tried by the known procedures of courts of justice and convicted by settled rules previously enacted, rather than according to the considerations of policy which moved legislative bodies.

There are three points which on their face might challenge that explanation of the origin of the American doctrine. One is that most of the arguments sought to differentiate legislative and executive powers but did not refer expressly to "judicial power." Professor Wormuth tells us of one commentary that did mention all three powers but he gives it little substance. John Sadler wrote in 1649 that he would extend the "sacred Trinity" to bodies politic and assign the institutional trio of Commons, Lords and King, a corresponding set of legal processes or functions—

original (or legislative), judicial and executive. Professor Wormuth calls this "curious analysis" a "political sport," pointing out that the classification of powers which emerged from the civil war period was that of legislative and executive, that those two terms served the republican cause against the monarchy even into the next century, and that the general assumption that laws should and would control particular actions supported the claim of parliamentary superiority.[7]   Both Professors Wormuth and Gwyn place primary emphasis upon the distinction between legislative and applicative functions and in that context "executive" may stand for both types of application. This analysis also indicates that the separate power doctrine involves a restricted concept of "executive power," that is, a legislatively limited authority.

The immediate point here is that in the rhetoric of the 1645-49 conflict, "executive power" was assumed to include judicial action[8] even though the courts had an accepted measure of operating independence. The process of eventual recognition of the separation of the judicial branch from the executive may be a precedent in form and substance for the present-day recognition of separate or coordinate presidential and administrative forces within the formal executive branch.[9]

Another outward difficulty with the proposition that the separate function maxim arose in arguments against the efforts of the Commons to enforce criminal laws is that Parliament at the time was deemed to be a court more than a legislature.[10]   However, its function as a "court"—a title consistent with the medieval notion that mortal beings might find or apply law but could not "make" it--was to review and possibly redress disturbing actions of judges and other officials. Hence, although this is rarely made clear, Parliament served more like an appellate court than a trial court. In the case of impeachment, a trial would be by the Lords, and in 1649 they did not participate in the Rump Parliament trial of the King.[11]   Likewise, Parliament's position as the "grand inquest" of governmental actions was similar in a general way to that of an appellate tribunal; if the Commons itself undertook to apply laws, it could not act properly in the capacity of a reviewing body.[12]

The third possible challenge to the English civil war theory of origin is that constitutional arrangement did not stabilize, even in a relative sense, until the revolution of 1688 and the declarations of 1689 and 1701. Professor Murray Dry makes this contention in his comprehensive review of the studies by Professors Gwyn and Vile.[13] However, at this point our interest, like that of Professors Wormuth, Gwyn and Vile, is much more in the intellectual origin of the doctrine than in its political acceptance. As a matter of fact, the separation of powers never did become a continuing constititional principle in England, even after the revolution. A half century later there were incidental references to it in the writings of Bolingbroke and Montesquieu,[14] but the distributional pattern which John Locke finally settled upon is the tripartite legislature of King, Lords and Commons, and that became the British idea of a balanced constitution.[15]

It is also Montesquieu's final and much less known trio of powers in (the fifty-fifth paragraph of) his chapter on the constitution of England.

Accordingly, these difficulties present no overwhelming obstacle to acceptance of the proposition that the separation doctrine originated in the English civil war period. Its association with the criminal law process indicates that the separate power principle may relate to only that limited area of operations. But it still has fundamental relevance. The criminal law process is even now the peculiar essence of government.[16] In the penal area, separate action by each of the three branches is still required, that is, there must be enactment of a criminal statute to be applied in particular situations, executive prosecution and some action by the judiciary prerequisite to coercive punishment. That interdependence of separate functions has a long history and is widely accepted in Anglo-American society. It is that inherent interdependence of functions and not the mere separation of institutions which works against potential tyranny.

When a single institution invokes the separate power doctrine in a situation where there is no such interdependence of functions, it may be able to make the principle appear to justify an unbalanced or undue concentration of authority. We may see this in three periods of strong antagonism between a chief executive and a legislative assembly. The period in which the rhetoric and the ideology of the doctrine arose clearly was more bitter than the English Revolution of 1688 or anything in Britain since then. First the King and then the Commons tried to rule alone. Secondly, the doctrine developed new force during the American colonial period in the confrontation of elected assemblies and royal governors. Many Americans came to assume that separate powers meant legislative supremacy. Eight of the nine new state constitutions of 1776-78 reflected that approach.[17] Only New York called for an elected governor, while Pennsylvania had only an executive council, and the others provided for legislative selection of the chief executive. Four of these last even had express declarations of the separate power doctrine.[18] Presumably they saw no inconsistency in the subordination of the chief executive. Later Massachusetts and New Hampshire adopted elected-governor systems.

The national convention of 1787 developed a more balanced arrangement. The majority of delegates, unlike Madison, apparently did not fear legislative supremacy, but eventually they allowed the president a partial veto power and approved a presidential selection method which left most discretion in the state legislatures.

The third period of separate power antagonism began with the presidency of Andrew Jackson. During the previous thirty years there had been more integration than separation in legislative-executive relationships despite the conflicts in John Adams's term and in 1810.[19] Jackson's intensification of congressional-presidential antagonism is a familiar story.[20] Thereafter we have had alternating periods of White House and

Capitol Hill supremacy. The flexibility in the meanings of legislative, executive or judicial, allows a particular branch with the requisite skill, strength and inclination to assert a dominant position contrary to the basic objective of the constitutional principle of interdependent authority. President Nixon used--or misused--the separation doctrine to defend excessive measures of "executive privilege," that is, the right to act alone in secrecy.

The Pure Theory of the American Doctrine

The initial clauses of the first three articles of the Constitution of the United States are the most unmixed expression of the separation doctrine in the national official documents. Those simple provisions furnish two sets of labels: one for institutions, that is, Congress, the president and the courts; and another for functions, that is, legislative, executive and judicial processes. Together, they raise three possible objectives, that is, separation of institutions, separation of functions, and parallel separation of institutions and functions. The last is the strictest and most ideological interpretation, and the one which most distinguishes the American doctrine from other allocation patterns.

The general political science explanations of American national government give limited attention to the strict meaning of the separation doctrine itself. Some mention the best known remarks of Montesquieu and Madison without critical analysis; a few contrast American and British constitutionalism with emphasis upon the differences between presidential and parliamentary government; but most explanations (like the analyses of Montesquieu and Madison) move from separation to checks and balances and stress mixed or shared functions more than separate ones. In this chapter, we are endeavoring to look at the separate function principle by itself.

The professor-authors of the most scholarly investigations and analyses of the theory of separate legislative, executive and judicial powers, distinguish that doctrine from other patterns of constitutional arrangement, such as mixed government, balanced constitution and limitation of powers.[21] Professors Wormuth and Gwyn place definite emphasis upon the idea that government consists of legal processes. They differentiate legislative action, on the one hand, and executive and judicial action, on the other hand.[22] That distinction embodies the implicit premise that general rules control particular orders. "The separation of powers was a corollary of the proposition that law is necessarily general and prospective."[23] When judges legislate, Professor Wormuth declares, we have "a breakdown of the separation of powers."[24] Professor Gwyn also stresses the distinction "between law-making and the implementation of the law in particular instances."[25] That distinction may be easier to maintain in the traditional fields of law, such as the criminal process, than in the complex newer areas where professional and technical specialists determine much policy in the process of application.

Professor Vile connects legislative supremacy with representative or popular sovereignty and considers the objective of the separation doctrine to be a manifestation of democracy. He finds the foremost application in the Pennsylvania Constitution of 1776; it provided for a unicameral legislature and no governor. [26]

The term "powers" has diverse significations. Professor Vile identifies five meanings of the word. In simple terms, these are persuasive influence, legal authority, governmental agency, legal function, and unit of personnel. [27] We will add a sixth--the political or social source of institutional authority. That meaning is essential to the classical concept of mixed government and the English ideas of balanced constitution. The American notion of the separation doctrine tends to avoid the political class meaning of "powers" suggested by the terms "monarchy" and "aristocracy" and to focus upon meanings which have a legalistic connotation. That is compatible with the beliefs that there are no classes in the United States and that our government conforms to legal or moral standards. Yet the separate power doctrine often is used as a pseudo-legal justification for political conflicts between Congress and the president as well as for the inability to resolve the differences between the two institutions.

This one-to-one correspondence between three functions and three institutions, declared in the initial clauses of Articles I, II and III of the Constitution, is an essential feature of what Professor Vile calls the "pure doctrine" of the separation of powers. [28] That theory has, he explains, three elements. The first is "that the government be divided into branches;" the second is that to each of the branches "there is a corresponding identifiable function of government, legislative, executive or judicial;" and the third is that "the persons who compose the three agencies of government must be kept separate and distinct, no individual being allowed to be at the same time a member of more than one branch."

The third may seem to support or even embody the first, but it need not be derived from the initial clauses of Articles I and II, because there is an express prohibition in the Constitution against members of Congress holding other positions. [29] That principle originated in English political struggles, specifically the rather vain efforts to protect the representative integrity of Parliament by restraining executive placement. We will see later in this chapter that similar provisions were common in the early state constitutions and even in the Articles of Confederation.

American constitutions from the start have been much better examples of mixed powers than of separate functions. Even those early state charters which included express declarations of the separate power doctrine--Virginia, Maryland, North Carolina and Georgia--provided for legislative selection of the governor and other high officials. [30] The national constitution also prescribed mixed allocations. The relevant Madison letters of The Federalist (47, 48, 51) sought to justify cross distribution much more than to advocate exclusive assignment of functions. Alexander Hamilton, in the New York ratification debates, asserted: "The legislative authority is lodged in three distinct branches, properly *balanced*; the executive is divided between two branches"[31] (presumably the presidency and the Senate). His Federalist letters 66 and 75 called attention to the "intermixture" in such matters as the adoption of treaties.

The Supreme Court has found ways of supporting both the theory of pure separation and the practice of flexible mixture. Justice Samuel Chase said in 1800 that "even in the constitution itself, we may trace repeated departures from the theoretical doctrine, that the legislative, executive and judicial powers, should be kept separate and distinct."[32] Later, the Supreme Court, under the Federalist leadership of John Marshall and Joseph Story, drew upon the maxim of separate, exclusive functions to raise the position of the national judiciary in relation to the legislative and executive powers as well as to the state courts. The main import of Marbury v. Madison (1803) was that the Court rather than Congress and the president has the supreme authority to determine the constitutional limits of the legislative power.

Later, Justices Story and Marshall made express applications of the exclusive function element of the separate power doctrine, in contrast to the shared function essence of checks and balances. Justice Story, in an 1816 case for which Marshall disqualified himself but probably approved of the result, treated the three vesting clauses as a conceptual unit and used the parallel allocation formula to enhance the position of the Court. Justice Story's opinion laid down a principle, now assumed but then disputed, that the national judiciary has a right to hear cases which arose in the state courts. "The object of the constitution," Story explained, "was to establish three great departments of government; the legislative, the executive and the judicial departments. The first was to pass laws, the second to approve and execute them, and the third to expound and enforce them. Without the latter it would be impossible to carry into effect some of the express provisions of the constitution."[33] This last sentence was Story's basis for asserting that the Court necessarily has the full measure of judicial power defined in the Constitution. John Marshall made a similar assertion in an 1824 opinion.[34] Later the Court held that Congress could authorize courts less than the total constitutionally defined judicial power.

The simplest statement of the threefold formula of parallel allocation is in Marshall's opinion in Wayman v. Southard (1825). The issue there was whether state laws on the execution of judgments applied in the federal courts and that turned in part on the authority of Congress to grant the federal courts the right to promulgate rules of procedure which Congress itself could have enacted.

Chief Justice Marshall set forth in the Wayman opinion that "the legislature makes, the executive executes and the judiciary construes the law" and concluded that the congressional grant of rule making authority to the federal courts was not invalid because Congress had not delegated what is "strictly and exclusively legislative."[35]   The decision aided the national judiciary against the states and the opinion preserved the theory of separate, exclusive functions, by reserving an undefined concept of "strictly and exclusively legislative."   That may pertain to only the criminal law processes.   If so, the doctrine of three-branch-separate-function government would not be applicable to the vast non-criminal field of operations.

The Supreme Court in the 1920s, when former President Taft was Chief Justice, held that it was for the executive alone to remove "political" appointees and to name the directors of government corporations.[36] Subsequently, the Court has not favored separate, exclusive powers.   For instance, in 1949 it held that Congress has not trespassed improperly upon the judicial branch in granting citizens of the District of Columbia the state citizenship necessary to sue in the federal courts.[37]   The Court said that the separate power doctrine was "fundamental" and "permeative" but apparently assumed that it embodied interaction.   Then in 1952 the famous steel seizure case held the presidency limited by specific congressional action; that is, President Truman lacked authority to order seizure of strike-threatened steel mills during the Korean war when he did not follow the labor relations procedure in the Taft-Hartley Act.   A concurring opinion said that the Constitution enjoins upon the branches of the government "separateness but interdependence, autonomy but reciprocity."[38]

Likewise, the Supreme Court has held that the separation doctrine does not prevent the judiciary from passing upon issues related to the essential autonomy of the legislative and executive branches.   In 1962, it declared that the federal courts had jurisdiction of controversies involving apportionment of legislative representation, overruling a previous position that that was a "political" matter.   In 1969, the Court held that the House of Representatives, in excluding a re-elected Congressman, acted unlawfully despite the express constitutional authority of each house to judge the qualifications of its own members.   Then, in 1974, it held that President Nixon could not retain, against a criminal law subpoena, the tapes of certain confidential conversations with his assistants.   These cases may have concerned issues of jurisdiction, standing or justiciability more directly than the separation doctrine, but in the last one the Court said that the denial of judicial authority to pass on the issue "would be contrary to the basic concept of separation of powers and the checks and balances that flow from the scheme of tripartite government."[39]   The joinder of the two principles would seem to provide an exceptionally flexible basis upon which to determine what is constitutionally proper in the allocation of functions among different institutions.

Where the Supreme Court has approved the most extensive departures from the pattern of exclusive functions has been in the delegation by Congress of rule-making authority to specialized administrators in non-criminal fields of legislation and adjudication.   The ways in which the

Court has endeavored to reconcile the dispersion of functions with the separate power doctrine will be considered in the ensuing sections.

Congressional Legislative Power

The reconciliation of the actual operations of the United States government with the "pure" doctrine of three institutions with separate functions might be a study in ideological transcendence, constitutional reductionism, metaphorical rhetoric, or classificatory abstraction if some one took the pains to analyze it in full degree, but not even political scientists seem that interested. As a consequence, we have in this matter little more than pragmatic answers to a limited number of particular issues.

The best record is in the Supreme Court because, more than any other institution, it strives for consistency and continuity, having a deep sense of identity with the past and future actions of the Court. However, its performance may raise more questions than it answers. In 1800 an opinion by Justice William Paterson, who had been the leading New Jersey delegate at the 1787 Constitutional Convention, set forth an inclusive definition of legislative power. He probably had state legislatures in mind when he said that "wherever the legislative power of a government is undefined, it includes the judicial and executive attributes." [40] Now we are more likely to define executive power that way. Chief Justice John Marshall suggested simple allocation in a noted 1810 opinion when he stated that "to the legislature all legislative power is granted." [41] However, in the particular case, the Court held that the Georgia legislature had contracted and not legislated when a few years previously it had granted tracts of land. That finding allowed the Court to decide that the contract provision of the national constitution prohibited Georgia from rescinding the grants even though they may have been tainted with fraud. Marshall admitted the lack of definitive meanings for the key terms and anticipated the case-to-case determination of separation issues when he said that there is no clear answer to "how far the power of giving the law may involve every other power" when the Constitution is silent on the matter. [42]

In 1825, Marshall's opinion in Wayman v. Southard[43] which, as we noted previously, set forth the ideal formula that "the legislature makes, the executive executes, and the judiciary construes the law," spelled out a complementary or perhaps counteracting principle that has allowed the whole range of governmental institutions to participate substantially and many times with practical finality in the legislative process. The opinion preserved the theory of legislative sovereignty in Congress by declaring that it must keep to itself "powers which are strictly and exclusively legislative" but at the same time opened the door for mixed legislative efforts by recognizing that Congress may delegate to others "powers which the legislature may rightfully exercise itself." He did not attempt to mark out the boundary and in fact acknowledged its uncertainty. "The line has not been exactly drawn which separates those important subjects, which must be entirely regulated by the legislature itself, from those of less interest, in which a general provision may be made, and power given to those who are to act under such general provisions to fill up the details." [44]   The particular case involved rule making by the courts for their own procedure, but the formula of leaving the "details" to other institutions can justify in equal manner congressional delegations to administrative bureaus of the authority to promulgate regulations which can and do serve as law.[45]

The Supreme Court has never specified the meaning of "strictly and exclusively legislative," at least not expressly or directly, and probably never will in a definitive way, but it has continued to approve diverse extensions of law-making power to executive and administrative units. For instance, in 1892 the Court held that a Congressional grant of power to the President to revise import duties was proper. At the same time, the Court maintained the doctrine or myth of legislative exclusiveness in Congress. "That Congress cannot delegate legislative power to the President," the Court said, "is a principle universally recognized as vital to the integrity and maintenance of the system of government ordained by the Constitution." [46]   In 1912, a typical opinion said that "Congress may not delegate its purely legislative power" but that "having laid down the general rules of action," Congress may require an administrative agency to make regulatory orders within such rules. [47]   Then, in the 1930s the Court disapproved of some of the New Deal recovery legislation, part of which delegated code-making authority to private associations. [48]   Otherwise the Supreme Court has not held invalid a delegation to an official governmental agency, even approving in 1947 a statute without explicit standards and in 1950 a delegation which may have resulted in individual rights being abridged by administrative regulations.[49]

There may be a limitation on congressional delegation to administrative agencies that has not been tested directly and definitely. When Congress has given a regulatory agency the power to issue subpoenas, it has placed final enforcement authority in the courts, and there is an indication that judicial finality is a constitutional requirement.[50]

The extent to which Congress has allowed specialized administrators to determine regulatory rules means that the legislative executive process has become reversed in many instances. Congress often is reduced to exercising a "veto" over the regulations promulgated by administrative authorities. If Congress can revise or remove such administrative legislation only by enactment of a statute, both houses must agree, not to having the rules, but to removing or amending them. If the president vetoes the statute, each must agree by two-thirds vote. Thus, bicameralism, or tripartitism, works to retain unwanted legislation rather than to prevent it. Since 1973, Congress has endeavored increasingly to counter this reversal of constitutional intent by inserting in laws delegating general authority a provision that proposed regulations can be vetoed by either house of Congress. This would avoid presidential veto as well as giving

Congress a stronger revisionary power. The reservation of a negative in each chamber makes congressional action on legislation developed by administrative forces tentative rather than final. The constitutional issues now are before the courts.[51]

There is a corollary to the substantive principle that Congress is not the only legislative institution; that is, that enactment of legislation is not the only function of Congress. Here again, the Supreme Court furnished the requisite constitutional support. The first step probably was an 1821 decision that each house of Congress has inherent authority to have its sergeant-in-arms detain a person who interferes with the orderly procedure of its activities.[52] Thus, it may engage in certain enforcement or executive functions. The misconduct in that case probably was attempted bribery, but the decision became a basis of investigative power, a matter on which the Constitution is silent. The power to deal with contemptuous persons supports the detention of witnesses who refuse to provide testimony without valid justification. In addition, Congress in 1857 enacted a statute under which refusal to answer a question pertinent to a matter under inquiry is a criminal offense.[53] This permits judicial trial of violations. The Court in 1881 held invalid a Congressional action against a recusant witness, but that judicial decision may have reflected the general trend at the time against specific actions by legislative bodies. In the particular case, the Court held that a Congressional committee had no legitimate objective in requiring the testimony of a private person about a bankruptcy transaction in which the Navy department was involved. The Court said that the inquiry was "clearly judicial" and that Congress had no authority to inquire into private matters.[54] However, half a century later, in 1927 to be exact, the Court held that a house of Congress could subpoena the brother of a former Attorney General with respect to transactions involving public lands. The Court found a legitimate purpose in the fact that the information might be an aid to the consideration of legislative proposals.[55] Thus, the Supreme Court preserved in theory the ideological maxim that the purpose of Congress is simply to legislate.

That decision and others in ensuing years opened the investigative door widely and now properly authorized committees of Congress may examine administrative officials (excluding some presidential advisers in the Executive Office) on almost any specific operation undertaken by a department or agency of the national government. The 1957 case in which the Supreme Court held that the witness rightfully refused to answer concerned merely the pertinency of particular questions rather than the basic authority of Congress and it involved the testimony of private persons rather than government officials.[56] Moreover, a 1959 decision held against a recusant witness on similar facts.[57] The latter opinion said that Congress may investigate only into "those areas in which it may potentially legislate or appropriate," thereby indicating that the limits of constitutional legislation and appropriation are not the same, and that investigation may be as broad as the others combined. In practice, investigation is likely to be primary in time as well as in scope.

Political scientists increasingly have said that Congress has functions other than legislation, including the "vigilant oversight of administration," informing the public, [58] and "providing representation for several kinds of clientage." [59]   These other powers may derive from or support the authority to legislate, but such powers as appropriation, investigation, communication, and surveillance, even if they serve the legislative role, constitute much of the actual activity of the congressional units. They also involve administrative officials in much of the broadened legislative process.

Accordingly, the congressional-administrative relationships are a complex matter. The separate function doctrine may have some restrictive effect upon those relationships but it seems to be limited to criminal law processes. This might have been what John Marshall intended by "strictly and exclusively legislative."   Actually Congress has allowed administrative units to engage in more and more specialized legislation and adjudication in non-criminal fields.

Presidential Executive Power

The clause vesting "executive power" in a president is, fortunately, not the only basis of presidential power—other sources include specific constitutional grants, statutory authorizations, and the inherent character of the presidency.   However, the "executive power" clause is our immediate concern.   The signification of the clause varies with our view of the constitutional context.   We note three approaches here: One is to consider the clause by itself—unsound as interpretative method and uncertain in result since taken alone "executive power" has meanings which range from ministerial to monarchical. Next, we may look at the clause in conjunction with the other vesting clauses and derive the Marshall formula which limits the executive to executing the laws made by the legislature. [60] The third approach is to view the clause with the specific constitutional prescriptions and develop a mixed or shared concept of the presidency. This last seems to be the soundest method, and we will examine the product in the next two chapters.

Here we will consider the second approach because we are endeavoring to measure the scope of the pure doctrine of separation of powers as indicated by the initial clauses of Articles I, II and III of the Constitution.   We will see that this makes the president more a policy enforcer than a policy formulator, but there is an appreciable amount of evidence that the majority of the delegations at the Constitutional Convention—in contrast to the views of Alexander Hamilton, James Madison, James Wilson and Gouveneur Morris—held such a restricted concept of the office.

The principal reasons for proposing a new constitution were to authorize the national government to impose tax and regulatory liabilities upon individuals within the states and to have national rather than state

35

officials for the enforcement of such obligations. That would decrease or maybe even end the unfortunate dependence of the central government upon the provincial attitudes of many state legislatures.[61] Governor Edmund Randolph made this clear at the start of the 1787 Convention when he explained the Virginia plan for a national legislature, executive and judiciary. "The Executive and Judiciary of the States, notwithstanding their nominal independence on the State Legislatures," he said, "are in fact so dependent on them, that unless they be brought under some tie to the National System, they will always lean too much on the State systems, whenever a contest arises between the two" (June 11, 1787). His later statements that the three national institutions should be separate in order to avoid concentration of authority is further indication that he thought of the national executive in relation to the coercive potential in the collection of taxes and the enforcement of regulations. The central government needed its own agencies of application, prosecution and adjudication if it was to attain governmental responsibility among the family of nations. [62]

The Constitution took some executive power from the states and gave it to Congress and the presidency. The first article authorizes Congress to enact laws necessary and proper for "carrying into execution" the powers of the government and the departments and officers. The second article vests the executive power in a president and grants that officer specific executive powers. The interaction of these provisions is a prime instance of the principle of checks and balances which we will analyze in the next chapter.

The extent to which some delegates at the 1787 Convention favored legislative supremacy is evident in the remark of Roger Sherman that "he considered the Executive magistracy as nothing more than an institution for carrying the will of the Legislature into effect" (June 1). Many other delegates probably had similar views. The nationalist sponsors of the Convention sought an executive which answered to the national legislature rather than to the state assemblies. The majority of the states favored legislative superiority, and the choice of the title "president" by the national convention seems significant because at the time it suggested a less dominant position than even "governor." It usually stood for presiding officer, such as the President of the Confederation Congress or the President of the Senate under the new Constitution. In Pennsylvania at the time, the chief officer was the President of the Executive Council, with the status of first among equals.

There is also evidence that about two-thirds of the state delegations at the 1787 Convention favored congressional selection of the president until they had to decide on whether the houses of Congress should vote jointly or separately in making the choice. Three times the delegations voted for congressional selection without deciding on the method of voting.[63] Near the end of the Convention—on August 24th—they faced the issue and by a seven to four vote approved a joint ballot. That apparently caused some states to have second thoughts about congressional selection. In the debate Jonathan Dayton (N.J.) said that "a *joint* ballot would in fact give the appointment to one House." The lower chamber was to have sixty-five members in contrast to twenty-six in the Senate. Thus, the joint ballot would favor the larger states and would undercut the force of the great compromise on senatorial representation. The reaction led to the electoral college scheme, but even that, as devised by the Convention, left basic choices in legislative bodies. The state legislatures were to determine the method of choosing presidential electors, and the House of Representatives was to make the final choice when no candidate received a majority of the electors. Significantly, the number of electors was equivalent to the total members of the two houses, which would have made the choice under the August 24th decision. The vote in the House of Representatives would be one vote for each state, thus favoring the smaller states.[64] Hence, the electoral scheme embodies some of the counterbalance of bicameralism.

James Madison's demands for a strong presidency were aimed at a veto power which could check what he feared, that is, radical legislation in the more popular legislative assembly. He and James Wilson, who also had some conservative views, tried repeatedly for the adoption of a Council of Revision composed of judges and the executive for a revisionary veto upon legislation (June 4, 6, July 21, and August 15, 1787), but they never gained support of more than three states. At least nine delegates[65] argued that the Council of Revision violated the separation of the judiciary. That probably was the strongest expression at the Convention of the pure correspondence doctrine of separate powers.[66] It is also further evidence that the doctrine was more a counterweight in debate than a guiding principle, and it adds to the general impression that the concept of separate executive power held by the majority of delegates does not make for a strong, positive presidency.

The positions of Madison and Wilson, carefully considered, do not seem to support the preference of twentieth-century "liberal" journalists and scholars for an affirmatively activist chief executive.[67] Present day advocates of a forceful presidency often show interest in those Convention delegates, such as Gouveneur Morris, Madison and Wilson, who wanted a strong president. But they sought that strength as a protective check upon radical legislation. Moreover, they were a minority. The majority of delegations most of the time preferred legislative supremacy.[68] The adoption of the electoral college compromise late in the Convention embodied the mixed power of checks and balances. It allowed the state legislatures and the House of Representatives crucial roles in the processes of selecting presidents.

Morever, even Wilson may have had a narrow concept of "executive power" as distinct from presidential power. Wilson said that he "preferred a single magistrate, as giving most energy, dispatch, and responsibility to the office," but in the same speech (June 1) he also stated that "the only powers he conceived strictly Executive were those of executing the laws and appointing officers, not appertaining to and appointed by the legislature." Wilson seems to have assumed legislative supremacy because each of these functions requires prior statutory action. Moreover, each is dealt with in a specific grant which, under tenets of interpretation, have precedence over a general clause.

There is other evidence that Wilson considered the conduct of foreign relations to be outside "executive power." The Committee of Detail, of which he was a leading member, proposed that the Senate have the power to make treaties and to appoint ambassadors without any reference to the president. That proposal was part of the mid-Convention report which originated the clause vesting "executive power" first, "in a single person" and later "in a President." Near the close of the Convention the present shared arrangement was adopted. This is more indication that the specific grants give the president more authority than the vesting clause.

The uncertain signification of the vesting clause may provide a determined president an apparently constitutional foundation for overreaching the boundaries of the office. Developments relating to Korean and Vietnam wars show how the separate function theory may be used—or misused—to support an "imperial presidency" in foreign relations and also how the checks and balances principle is needed to bring the presidency within the basic constitutional pattern of shared or mixed powers.

A presidential claim of policy domination over the whole field of administrative operations is frequently defended on the basis of the Constitutional provision that the president "take care that the laws be faithfully executed," but that clause probably was intended to admonish the chief executive to be faithful to what Congress decreed as well as to authorize national enforcement. The clause hardly supports the type of partisan executive emphasized by many occupants of the presidential office. At the start of the 1787 Convention, the provision merely gave the right to execute national laws, and later the Committee of Detail added the "take care" responsibility for the faithful execution of the laws. The addition probably was an attempt to impose non-suspension of laws upon the chief executive as Parliament had done in Britain a century before. The first item in the English Bill of Rights of 1689 was "that the pretended power of suspending of laws or the execution of laws by regal authority without the consent of parliament is illegal."[69] When the Americans took their independence, six of the seven declarations of rights adopted by the new states during 1776-84 included express provisions that the executive should not suspend the application of laws without legislative consent.[70] The single exception was Pennsylvania, and its constitution did not provide for a governor. Even in Massachusetts, which had an annually elected governor, the Bill of Rights included an express clause prohibiting suspensions without the approval of the legislature. The clause in the Federal Constitution is much like parts of a provision in the 1777 New York Constitution.[71]

The Supreme Court first indicated that a president's duty under the "take care" clause was to see that officials acted honestly in applying the enacted laws and that he could not impose his own view of a statute. In 1838 the Court held that President Jackson could not suspend a ministerial duty imposed by Congress upon the Postmaster General, and it approved a writ of mandamus against that official. [72] But an 1840 decision held that mandamus would not lie where application involved "political" or "executive" discretion. [73] About the same time the position of department heads changed basically with the Senate's acquiesence in Jackson's repeated switching of his Secretary of the Treasury to obtain removal of the bank deposits. [74]

A half century later, the Supreme Court upheld wide enforcement power in the presidency. The Court took the position in an 1890 opinion that the right or duty under the clause was not limited to acts of Congress and treaties but applied also to obligations implied by the nature of the government under the Constitution. [75] The case concerned a United States marshall, named Neagle, who had shot a man in California while protecting a Supreme Court justice on circuit duty. The marshall's authority was no higher than the Attorney General's order to guard the justice. The Supreme Court denied California the right to prosecute the marshall on the ground that he was acting under "a law of the United States" for purposes of a national statute transferring the marshall from state to national custody. The decision suggests some degree of executive prerogative in areas of domestic order. No doubt there are limits upon any such authority and it may be supplemental. Many internal security matters, even of larger scope, are supported by statutory authorizations. For instance, there are long standing statutes authorizing presidential use of military forces in case of rebellion or insurrection.

The presidential administrative authority is sometimes based upon the "take care" clause, but it would seem to have limitations. The goal is "faithful execution," and that means fidelity to congressional legislative intent more than to presidential partisan policy. It would also seem to preclude impoundment of specific, nondiscretionary, appropriations. Pending court cases may or may not provide final answers.

The Neagle case indicates some degree of prerogative-like authority inherent in the presidency, in a departmental headship, and perhaps in other executive offices. In any event, the decision seems to lessen the need for relying upon the more debatable clauses of the Constitution. Likewise, it may contribute support for the inherent identify and legitimacy of the continuing administrative system.

Separate Integrity of Judicial Positions

The constitutional clauses vesting three types of power in three separate institutions seem particularly redundant in the situation of the judiciary. To say that "judicial power" is vested in courts is almost a truism because the two often are defined in terms of each other. Also, there are other constitutional provisions and inherent principles which support judicial independence in strong fashion. Moreover, the judiciary is not limited to the simple role of the Marshall formula; when the courts interpret the Constitution, they in effect may legislate rules for Congress to execute.

One of the most striking aspects of American beliefs about the judiciary, and this applies to social and political scientists as well as to journalists and the public, is that we think of the Supreme Court as the prime example of the judicial function when in fact it is highly atypical. The Supreme Court is not characteristic in several ways. For one thing, political and sociological or demographic factors enter into the appointment of the justices more definitely and more openly than for other judges so that the Supreme Court may be more like a politically representative body than other tribunals. The practice by which all nine members participate in most cases results in their dividing more or less into left, right and center blocs, and that tends to underscore their general representative character. The size, with three times as many judges acting on a case as in the next lower courts, adds to this phenomenon. The Supreme Court can also be much more selective in the cases or controversies to which it gives full consideration than can the other courts in the federal system.[76] Accordingly, it has a choice of subject matter and can pick out certain areas for the revision, adjustment or support of the law. In these respects it is more like a legislative institution than the usual judicial body which commonly decides such matters as the lawyers bring to it. The Supreme Court has used its considerable choice of cases to alter different realms of the law, moving successively from such areas as due process of law to the first amendment and the equal protection clause and then to its own judicial conception of fair trial. Accordingly, if the separate power doctrine means that the judiciary applies what the legislature prescribes, it seems to pertain much less to the Supreme Court than to career officials engaged in administrative adjudication.

The separate function doctrine may be more applicable to the inferior federal courts, particularly the district trial courts. They, to a much larger degree than the Supreme Court, apply law "made" by others. Yet their separation in matters of personnel, procedures and attitudes from Congress and the presidency may rest less upon the three-branch theory than upon long-standing concepts of established procedure and detached perspectives and standards. The judicial process developed by gradual accretion, fortified by extraordinary demands, such as those evidenced by the Magna Carta of 1215, the Petition of Right of 1628, the Bill of Rights of 1689, and the Resolves of the First Continental Congress of 1774.[77] The declarations of rights adopted by the newly independent American states during 1776-84 contained more provisions on criminal law procedure than on any other single matter.[78] Also, more than half of the specific clauses in the national bill of rights deal with that subject. If, as Professor Wormuth says, the first purpose of separate powers was to assure accused persons of trial by known procedures of justice and settled rules of law, then that objective may be protected much more certainly by the clauses of the Fourth, Fifth, Sixth, Eighth and Fourteenth Amendments than by the constitutional provisions vesting the three powers on a separate basis.

The distinctive character of the judicial branch concerns not only the types of procedure and the modes of decision but even more sharply the length of judicial tenure and the degree of protection against policy removal or replacement. These features developed in England well before the American independence. The king himself first established the common law courts and classified his own advisers and assistants, as early as the twelfth century.[79] He appointed the judges for the term of "his pleasure," but as time went on this was less and less a matter of personal whim or even factional politics. By 1600 the judges "had in practice security of tenure" and the bench was "independent" in fact if not in law,[80] as we noted in discussing the rise of the separation doctrine in the English civil war. Formal recognition came with the Settlement Act of 1701, which provided that judges be appointed for "good behavior," that is, legal propriety, subject to removal by joint action of the two houses of Parliament.[81] The historical process by which judges became independent of the king and by which the judiciary acquired separate status has similarities to the development within the past hundred years by which the civil servants in the United States government acquired legal independence from the politics of the presidency and became in substance at least a separate operating force within the American government.

Many colonial and state constitutions during the eighteenth century included provisions which differentiated between the responsibilities of judges and those of legislative and executive officials. The Pennsylvania Charter of Privileges (1701) expressly required those serving the government "in any capacity both legislatively and executively" to be Christian believers but made no such statement about judges.[82] Later, the new American state constitutions made implicit distinctions. Four of the five state declarations of rights promulgated in 1776 included provisions which set general standards for legislative and executive officials but which did not mention judges. Pennsylvania asserted that since all power derives from the people, "all officers of government, whether legislative or executive, are their trustees and servants." Maryland declared that "all persons invested with legislative or executive powers of government are trustees of the public," and Delaware had a similar provision.

Most interesting is the Virginia provision—in addition to the general statement on the separation of legislative, executive and judicial departments—that "the legislative and executive powers of the state should be separate and distinct from the judiciary" and that in order that "the members of the two first may be restrained from oppression, by feeling and participating the burdens of the people," they should at fixed intervals, "be reduced to a private station" and the vacancies filled "by frequent, certain and regular elections," in which the former members would be eligible or not as the laws direct.[83] Apparently, there was a general belief at the time that judges were sufficiently responsible to the law that it was not necessary or proper to require their periodic association with the tribulations of the people.

The Supreme Court, for more than a century, has asserted a type of distinction between the judiciary and the other two branches, in developing and adjusting the doctrine of nonjusticiable "political" questions. It has called the executive and legislative, the "political departments" and held that "the propriety of what may be done in the exercise of this political power is not subject to judicial inquiry."[84] In 1962 and 1969 landmark decisions concerning legislative apportionment and congressional membership, the Court altered its view of the scope of that disability. In doing so, it declared: "The nonjusticiability of a political question is primarily a function of the separation of powers."[85] However, the English courts also have refused to decide such questions, notably those on foreign affairs.[86] The record on "political questions" shows again that flexibility in the meaning of terms facilitates the expansion of the principles of authority distribution.

American constitutions from the start have made differences between the judiciary and the other two branches on the terms of office. The majority of state constitutions of 1776-84 followed the English development in giving judges definite security of tenure. Seven of the eleven states with new constitutions prescribed terms of "good behavior" for judges and the other states stipulated terms of at least five years. In contrast, no state legislative or executive officer had a specifed term of even five years. The majority of top offices had terms of only one year. The longest non-judicial term seems to have been four years for senators in New York and Virginia.[87] The national constitution adopted in 1789 was even more definite, expressly assuring judges terms of "good behavior" while prescribing two, six and four years for the three named types of legislative and executive officials. There is a comparability between the federal judges and the career civil servants which bears upon the propriety of the separate administrative branch.

The Constitution further supports the independence of judges by a specific prohibition against reductions in compensation during continuance in office. The Supreme Court has held that that provision exempted judges of the federal courts established to exercise "judicial power" as defined in Article III, from a government-wide reduction in salaries which Congress enacted as part of the Appropriation Act of 1932[88] even though the purpose of the enactment was to spread the burden of the depression among government employees and officials generally. The opinion referred to the separate power doctrine, but that seems to be dictum rather than a basis for the decision because at the same time the Court held that the salary reduction was applicable to the judges of a "legislative" court established solely under Article I.[89] The separate power doctrine cannot be the basis for the disability of Congress to reduce the salaries of federal judges because it did not prevent the legislative branch from scaling down the compensation of officials in the executive, administrative or quasi-judicial positions.

Accordingly, the separation of the judiciary rests upon a special foundation and one with more strength than the separate power doctrine.

The institutional separation expressed in the Constitution involves two types of relationship, that is, the comparative independence of the judiciary, established and maintained by traditional values, procedural norms and guaranteed tenure, and the comparative interdependence of the three "political" elected institutions which share the legislative authority and responsibility on a mutual-negative basis.[90]

Separate Integrity of Congressional Positions

The American system of power distribution differs from the parliamentary-cabinet government in England not only in the institutional independence of the presidency but also in the comparative freedom of the representative assemblies. The British plan features the deliberate integration of legislative and executive leaderships while the United States pattern involves essentially the constitutional separation and even the political antagonism of the two hierarchies.

That situation may result from constitutional provisions other than the vesting clauses at the start of the first three articles. There are more specific bases of both allocation and separation. The main body of the Constitution includes provisions which intermingle the functions of two institutions, such as the grant of a legislative veto to the president and the requirement that the Senate approve "superior" appointments by the president and any treaties negotiated by the executive. Moreover, the body of the Constitution also provides for the institutional separation of the Congress and the executive. There is an express direction, more specific than the vesting clauses, that "no Person holding any office under the United States, shall be a member of either House during his Continuance in Office."[91]

The history of such prohibitory provisions indicates an intent to protect the deliberative integrity of the legislatures from deleterious tactics by chief executives. That objective is evident from many facts in British political history, in American colonial governments, in the state constitutions of 1776-84 and in the Articles of Confederation as well as in the Constitution.

The British side of the story goes back to the seventeenth century. Often it is associated with the debatable activities of Robert Walpole, the King's chief minister during 1721-42, but similar practices occurred several decades earlier. In fact, the 1701 Act of Settlement declared, without enduring effect, "that no person who has an office or place or profit under the king or receives a pension from the crown shall be capable of serving as a member of the house of commons."[92] That formal prohibition did not stop the practice of the king or his minister from trying to control the House of Commons, not only by intervening in elections but also by "placing" members of Parliament in sinecure positions with the aim of gaining their support.[93] This is the opposite of the later parliamentary-cabinet system because in the earlier period the king selected the chief minister in substance as well as in form, and he did so with no necessary regard for the party lineup in the parliament.[94]

American disqualifications of members of an assembly for other offices antedate even the constitutions of 1776. A comparable provision appears in the 1732 charter for Georgia. There it concerned the members of the colonial corporation who met once a year to decide on general policy matters. The charter declared that any person who has "any place, office or employment of profit, under the said corporation, shall be incapable of being elected a member of the said corporation," and if one takes such a position, he ceases to be a member.[95] The prohibition extended to offices held in trust and this suggests suspicion of or perhaps prior experience with types of evasion.

The depth of feeling against representatives serving in other offices is evident in the minutes of the Journal of the Virginia General Convention during 1775. That was the interim provincial congress which undertook to govern the colony-state when military activities began and before the new constitution was adopted. The Journal shows that certain types of persons were ineligible to sit or to vote as members of the Convention. These included military officers, county and town corporation officials, "and clergymen of the Church of England and all dissenting ministers or teachers," and "any person who shall . . . . have procured himself to be elected by bribery, in giving money, or any publick entertainment of meat or drink, or made any promise to do so to the electors, or by any other corrupt practices."[96]

Each of the state constitutions drafted and adopted during 1776-84, after the first hasty New Hampshire constitution early in 1776, contained some kind of provision forbidding legislators from holding other offices. The temporary South Carolina constitution of March 1776 declared that if a member of the general assembly accepts "any place of emolument, or any commission except in the militia, he shall vacate his seat." In case of such a vacancy, there was to be a new election at which the member involved might run and if reelected could continue to serve. Presumably, the electorate had a more final say than the ethical principle involved. The Virginia Constitution of 1776 expressly prohibited any person, except a justice of peace, from exercising the powers of more than one of the legislative, executive and judiciary departments.[97] The New Jersey Constitution of July 1776 said that the reason for such a provision was to preserve the legislature from "suspicion of corruption."[98]

A number of the new state constitutions extended the exclusion beyond legislative-executive relationships. Pennsylvania barred certain types of officers from both the executive council and the general assembly. The Delaware constitution excluded from either house not only several types of officials but also "all persons concerned in any army or navy contracts," while the North Carolina prohibitions extended to clergymen and some other persons outside the government.[99] The Maryland and Georgia constitutions (of 1776 and 1777, respectively) included broad provisions against any person holding more than one office of profit at the same time, except that, in the latter instance, the constitution permitted officers of the militia and justices of the peace to be representatives. [100]

The general import of these various provisions seems to be in accord with both legislative supremacy and representative sovereignty. The apparent objective is not so much to separate the legislative and executive institutions as to maintain the deliberative integrity of the representative assemblies from a diversity of outside influences but most of all from efforts of chief executives to undermine the discretionary capacity of the legislators to act in the "public interest" as they see it. None of the provisions seems to spring from the doctrine of separate powers itself. Rather, they are aimed at middle-level conflicts of interest. Exceptions for local justices are frequent, and the majority of states authorized the legislatures to select the governors and other high officials.

Most interesting is the presence of such an exclusion in the Articles of Confederation. After limiting the tenure of any delegate of a state in Congress to three years in any six, the Articles prescribed that no delegate shall be capable of holding "any office under the United States" for which he or another for his benefit received "any salary or other emolument." [101] The mention of indirect compensation indicates that the drafters of the Articles were aware of possible loopholes and circumventions. Clearly, the provision in the Articles of Confederation was not to prevent legislative supervision of executive actions because there was no coordinate division of authority in the Articles, the whole power of ultimate control being in the Congress of state delegates. This suggests strongly that the inclusion of a similar provision in the Constitution of 1789 was not intended to prevent Congressional control of administrative action and may even have been intended to assure a high level of supervisory responsibility.

The provision in the Constitution adopted by the 1787 Convention was the result of a number of compromises. The relevant clause in the Virginia Plan at the start had extended ineligibility to state offices as well as national ones and the delegates first approved an extra year of disqualification. Later, each of these additions was eliminated. James Madison opposed any general limitation, apparently because it would weaken the bargaining power of the president with Congress. He tried to reduce the scope of the exclusion by limiting the ineligibility of members of the first branch to offices that had been established or improved during the period of membership. This, he said was the most evil practice experienced. Madison, most likely, was less concerned with protecting the future opportunities of members of Congress than with endeavoring to strengthen the hand of the chief executive in relation to the House of Representatives. John Francis Mercer of Maryland made an unusually frank statement of the nationalist position for a strong executive and the strategic or tactical use of the appointing power. "The Executive has not *force* , deprive him of influence by rendering the members of the Legislature ineligible to Executive Offices, and he becomes a mere phantom of authority," Mercer declared.[102] Yet the Convention did deny the presidency such power.

The constitutional ban against ·Senators and Representatives holding "offices under the United States" thus was apparently intended to protect legislative supremacy and integrity. The clause is another example of the manner in which the Convention dealt with institutional relationships by prescribing specific powers and limitations rather than by leaving such matters to the general import of the vesting clauses of the first three articles. Particularly relevant to this study, the constitutional prohibition does not prevent members of Congress from entering into the guidance of administration as long as they do not become executive officers at the same time. There seems to be no restriction of word or spirit upon their efforts to control administrators even in non-legislative ways. In fact, the aims of both representative democracy and government under law seem to require such congressional participation. Thus, the constitutional provision for the separation of legislative and executive personnel seems to provide no obstacle to the congressional efforts to make the specialized policy makers of the administrative branch the agents in effect of Congress in their various types of functions.[103]

Summary

This chapter has developed a number of ideas concerning the constitutional clauses vesting legislative, executive and judicial powers in Congress, a president and the courts, respectively. The main purpose of this three-branch-separate-function pattern is to make different persons determine the three principal types of criminal law processes in order to prevent undue concentration of coercive authority. The distinctive essence of the separate power doctrine concerns, not institutions, but functions. Separate institutions are preliminary to mixed powers and shared functions as well as to separate ones. The Constitution also provides in other ways with more specificity for the institutional separation of legislative, executive and judicial officials. For instance, there is a particular provision against members of Congress holding executive offices.

The capacity of separate institutions to prevent undue concentration of governmental power depends upon the allocation of functions among the branches. Three general patterns are possible: (1) exclusive functions with such established interdependence that legislation exerts specific controls, such as there is in criminal procedure where penal statutes must define offenses with more than average specificity and thus limit executive and judicial spheres of discretion; (2) constitutionally prescribed sharing or mixing of functions, such as the legislative process involving the houses of Congress and the presidency, the presidential-senatorial approval of treaties, and the congressional-presidential authorities on the appointment of officials; and (3) unshared functions without established interdependence, such as there may be in certain aspects of military and diplomatic matters. The first and second of these patterns may embody in general an effective degree of checks and balances. However, the third may not. This last involves some degree of disregard by Congress and the presidents of the extent to which the Constitution prescribes congressional authority and responsibility. Foreign affairs is the area where there is most likely to be a claim that separation of institutions justifies independence of functions even though properly institutional diversity is merely a means to functional interdependence.

The Supreme Court has in effect maintained the three-branch-separate-function pattern in the criminal law field, but in other areas it seems to have reduced considerably the scope and force of separate functions. While it has held that Congress cannot delegate what is "strictly and exclusively legislative," it has approved the delegation of almost no end of other legislative-like power to judicial, executive and administrative officials. The Court has not defined that special class of legislation but in effect it is the criminal law area. Congressional delegation to the specialized administrators has been vast, and it makes the administrative bureaucracy a mixed power force.

The clause vesting "executive power" in a president is an uncertain and even restrictive basis of authority. The three vesting clauses as a unit indicate a tripartite formula such as the one of Chief Justice Marshall that "the legislature makes, the executive executes and the judiciary construes the law." Today, the administrative force fits into that pattern much more definitely than does the presidential force. What the presidency does other than execute the laws made by Congress is sufficient for a whole branch of government in itself.

The immense growth of the formal executive branch since 1790, or even since 1890, suggests that its division into counteracting realms may be not only appropriate but also necessary if we are to attain the objectives of the constitutional principles of distributed authority, that is, to prevent undue concentration of power and to assure responsible exercise of authority. The executive functions are more diverse as well as larger in volume, and those undertaken by the presidential forces may be the more general, external functions, while those exercised by the administrative units are the more specialized and internal functions. The establishment of the Civil Service and other merit systems has accentuated this division by providing career orientation for the specialized professionals. The separation of the presidential and administrative forces may be unsystematic, but it is persistent, and there is much substance in the underlying, more-or-less horizontal division between the partisanly political officials of the presidential realm and the specialized policy professionals of the administrative bureaucracy. Constitutional distribution entails the structural identity of different institutions as a basis for operating interdependence, and the presidential-administrative separation serves that constitutional function.

NOTES

1.   When the delegates began on May 30, 1787 to consider the Virginia Plan and particularly the resolution that "a *national* Government ought to be established consisting of a *supreme* Legislative,   Executive and Judiciary," Charles Pinkney asked Governor Edmund Randolph "whether he meant ·to abolish the State Governments altogether." Later, on June 20, 1787, the Convention on a resolution by Oliver Ellsworth struck out the word "national" in such provisions in favor of "the United States."   The report July 26 to the Committee of Detail said the government ought to consist of "a supreme legislative, judiciary, and executive," while the report from the Committee spoke of "supreme legislative, executive and judicial powers."   The key term seems to be "supreme."   The provision was approved promptly without comment but apparently removed by the Committee of Style during the final days. Notes of Debates in the Federal Convention of 1787 Reported by James Madison New York: W.W. Norton (1969). Excerpts from the debates at various points in this study will be taken from this edition of Madison's journal; references will be to the date of the particular debate.
2.   Karl Loewenstein Political Power and the Governmental Process Chicago: University of Chicago Press, (1957) 42.
3.   Gordon S. Wood, The Creation of the American Republic 1776-1787 Chapel Hill: University of North Carolina Press, (1969) 151.
4.   Francis D. Wormuth The Origins of Modern Constitutionalism New York: Harper and Bros. (1949) 59-70; William Gwyn The Meaning of Separation of Powers New Orleans: Tulane University Press (1967) 28-65; M.J.C. Vile Constitutionalism and the Separation of Powers Oxford: Clarendon Press (1967) 39-51.
5.   Wormuth op. cit. 63-66.
6.   Ibid. 64.
7.   Ibid. 60-61, 62, 63-67, 89-97, 191-92, 211-12.
8.   "When the term judicial power was used, it was as a synonym for executive power rather than as a third function of government." Wormuth, op. cit. 62. "What we now call executive and judicial functions were known then usually as simply 'executive power.' " Gwyn op. cit. 5.
9.   See The Pure Theory of the American Doctrine infra.
10. "The work of the early Parliament consisted essentially of judicial functions."   Colin R. Lovell English Constitutional and Legal History New York: Oxford University Press (1962) 165.
11. Wormuth op. cit. 86-87.
12. "Parliament was thought of as an inquisitorial body for the supervision and correction of administration." · Wormuth op. cit. 65. See also Bryce Lyon A Constitutional and Legal History of Medieval England New York: Harper and Bros. (1960) 426, 595-98, 600-25.
13. Murray Dry "The Separation of Powers and Representative Government" 3 The Political Science Reviewer (Fall 1973) 43-83.
14. Vile op. cit. 72-75, 83-97; Gwyn op. cit. 101-17.
15. Gwyn op. cit. 100-1; Wormuth op. cit. 174, 179.
16. "All government involves coercion." Randall B. Ripley American National Government and Public Policy New York: Free Press -Macmillan (1974) 4.

17. Delaware (76), Georgia (77), Maryland (76), New Jersey (76), New York (77), North Carolina (76), Pennsylvania (76), South Carolina (76,78), Virginia (76) Benjamin Perley Poore (Ed.) The Federal and State Constitutions, Colonial Charters, and other Organic Laws of the United States Washington, D.C.: Government Printing Office (1877) 273-78, 377-83, 817-28, 1310-14, 1328-39, 1409-14, 1540-48, 1616-27, 1908-12.

18. Georgia, Maryland, North Carolina, Virginia, Poore. op. cit. 378, 818, 1409, 1910.

19. "In brief, the initiation and preparation of legislation for the consideration of the House during the Federalist administrations were to be the business of 'ministers' as it is in the British parliamentary system to this day, . . ." Wilfred E. Binkley President and Congress New York: Alfred A. Knopf (1047) 33. President Jefferson's Secretary of the Treasury, Albert Gallatin, "seems to have been almost as active as Hamilton had been in steering measures through Congress . . . . By 1808 the caucus had become powerful enough to pass from being an instrument for executive control of Congress and start on its career of the control of the Executive." Ibid. 54, 55.

20. Ibid. 66, 86, 283-99. "Jackson is variously said to have restored, remade the presidency, or to have been the first real President." Grant McConnell The Modern Presidency New York: St. Martin's (1967) 9; Second Edition (1976) 12.

21. Vile op. cit. 33, 93, 99, 136. "There is no medieval doctrine of the separation of powers, though there is a very definite doctrine of limitation of powers." C.H. McIlwain Constitutionalism Ancient and Modern Ithaca, N.Y.: Cornell University Press (1947) 142.

22. Wormuth op. cit. 62, 67, 191-92; Gwyn op. cit. 5, 13.

23. Wormuth op. cit. 193, 205.

24. Ibid. 205.

25. Gwyn op. cit. 5.

26. Vile op. cit. 136, 138.

27. Ibid. 12.

28. Ibid. 13-18.

29. See infra Separate Integrity of Congressional Positions.

30. See fn. 18, supra; see also Kentucky Constitution of 1798 and Illinois Constitution of 1818, Poore op. cit. 657 and 440.

31. Jonathan Elliot The Debates in the Several State Conventions Philadelphia: J.B. Lippincott (1861) II, 348.

32. Cooper v. Telfair 4 Dall. 14, 15-16 (1800).

33. Martin v. Hunter's Lessee 1 Wheat. 304, 328 (1816).

34. Osborn v. The Bank of the United States 9 Wheat. 738, 819 (1824)

35. Wayman v. Southard 10 Wheat. 1, 42, 46 (1825).

36. Myers v. United States 272 U.S. 52 (1926) and Springer v. Philippine Islands 277 U.S. 189, 201-209, 211, 212 (1928).

37. National Mutual Insurance Co., v. Tidewater Transfer Co. 337 U.S. 582 (1949) at 590-91; see also 628.

38. Youngstown Co. v. Sawyer 343 U.S. 579 (1952) opinion of Justice Jackson, Ibid. 635.

39. Baker v. Carr 369 U.S. 186 (1962); Powell v. McCormack 395 U.S. 486 (1969); and U.S. v. Nixon 418 U.S. 683, 704 (1974). This last is dis-

cussed in The Wide Scope of Mixed Power Government--The Shared Duty to Cooperate.

40. Cooper v. Telfair 4 Dall. 14 (1800) at 19.
41. Fletcher v. Peck 6 Cranch 87 (1810).
42. Ibid. 136.
43. Wayman v. Southard 10 Wheat. 1, 46. (1825).
44. Ibid. 42, 43.
45. See generally G. Burdeau "Delegation of Powers," International Encyclopedia of the Social Sciences New York: Macmillan (1968); Kenneth Culp Davis Administrative Law and Government St. Paul: West Publishing Co., (1960) 68-71.
46. Field v. Clark 143 U.S. 649, 692 (1892).
47. Interstate Commerce Commission v. Goodrich Transit Co. 224 U.S. 194, 214 (1912).
48. Schechter v. U.S. 295 U.S. 495 (1935); Panama Refining Co. v. Ryan 293 U.S. 388 (1935).
49. Fahey v. Mallonee 332 U.S. 245 (1947). Knauff v. Shaughnessy 338 U.S. 537 (1950) and Zemel v. Rusk 381 U.S. 1 (1965).
50. There may be dicta to this effect in Interstate Commerce Commission v. Brimson 154 U.S. 447 (1894). That case approved the use of the contempt power of the courts to aid the enforcement of I.C.C. orders.
51. "Congressional Veto: Constitutionality Challenged," 34 Congressional Quarterly (July 31, 1976) 2029-31. See also fn. 103, infra.
52. Anderson v. Dunn 6 Wheat. 204 (1821).
53. 2. U.S. Code 191; 5. Stat. L. 115.
54. Kilbourn v. Thompson 103 U.S. 168, 192 (1881).
55. McGrain v. Daugherty 273 U.S. 135, 190 (1927).
56. Watkins v. United States 354 U.S. 178 (1957).
57. Barenblatt v. United States 360 U.S. 109, 111, 112 (1959).
58. Woodrow Wilson Congressional Government Boston: Houghton Mifflin (1885, 1891) 297, 303.
59. William J. Keefe and Morris Ogul The American Legislative Process: Congress and the States Third Edition, Englewood Cliffs, N.J.: Prentice-Hall (1973) 12. John S. Saloma III Congress and the New Politics Boston: Little, Brown (1969) 22-23 lists eleven specific functions and seven general ones.
60. See fn. 43 supra.
61. Six of the seven constitutions adopted in 1776 provided for legislative selection of the executive—South Carolina, Virginia, Maryland, Delaware, North Carolina and New Jersey. Pennsylvania omitted the office of a single chief executive. The Georgia constitution (1777) and the second South Carolina one (1778) also authorized legislative selection of the governor. The constitutions of New York (1777), Massachusetts (1780) and New Hampshire (1784) each called for an elected chief executive. "But even though the new governors and judges were to be elective, there remained a much greater confidence in the legislative branch of government than in the executive or judiciary." Edmund S. Morgan The Birth of the Republic 1763-1789. Chicago: University of Chicago Press (1956) 92.

62. "The problem then was to construct a representative government of divided powers on the model of the state governments but without the flaws which ten years' wear and tear had brought to light." Morgan op. cit. 138. See also John Roche "Constitutional Law: Distribution of Powers," International Encyclopedia of the Social Sciences New York: Macmillan (1968) III, 305.

63. In The Committee of the Whole, June 2, 1787 and July 17, 787; and in Convention July 26, 1787.

64. See generally, Joseph Kallenbach The American Chief Executive New York: Harper and Row (1966) 47-49.

65. Bedford, Dickenson, Gerry, Ghorum, King, Martin, Pinkney, Rutledge and Strong, June 4, 6, July 21, and August 15, 1787.

66. For instance, Caleb Strong on July 21, 1787 said that "the power of making ought to be kept distinct from that of expounding, the laws. No maxim was better established. The Judges in exercising the function of expositors might be influenced by the part they had taken, in framing the laws."

67. See Malcolm P. Sharp "The Classical American Doctrine of 'The Separation of Powers'," 2 University of Chicago Law Review 385-456 and Arthur T. Vanderbilt The Doctrine of Separation of Powers Lincoln, Neb.: University of Nebraska Press (1953).

68. See Forrest MacDonald E Pluribus Unum: The Formation of the American Republic 1776-1790 Boston: Houghton Mifflin (1965) 184-86.

69. Carl Stephenson and Frederick G. Marcham Sources of English Constitutional History New York: Harper and Bros. (1937) 601.

70. Delaware, Maryland, Massachusetts, New Hampshire, North Carolina, Virginia. Poore op. cit. 818, 959, 1283, 1409, 1909.

71. Ibid. 1335.

72. Kendall v. United States 12 Peters 524, 618 (1838).

73. For instance, United States v. Eliason 16 Peters 291, 302 (1842).

74. See Rowland Egger The President of the United States Second Edition New York: McGraw-Hill (1972) 33-35.

75. In re Neagle 135 U.S. 1, 59 (1890) See Edward S. Corwin The President: Office and Powers Third Edition, New York: New York University Press (1948) 182-88.

76. Sheldon Goldman and Thomas P. Janige The Federal Courts as a Political System New York: Harper and Row (1971) 28-33, 128-31, 205-213.

77. Stephenson and Marcham op. cit. 115, 453 and 599; Henry S. Commager Documents of American History Fifth Edition New York: Appleton-Century-Crofts (1949) I, 82.

78. See, for instance, the Virginia and Massachusetts bills of rights, Commager, op. cit. I, 103, 107.

79. Lovell op. cit. 85-91.

80. Ibid. 328.

81. Stephenson and Marcham op. cit. 612.

82. Poore op. cit. 1537.

83. Ibid. 1541, 817, 1909.

84. Oetjen v. Central Leather Co. 246 U.S. 297 (1918) at 302.

85. Baker v. Carr 369 U.S. 186 (1962) at 210; Powell v. McCormack 395 U.S. 486 (1969) 512, 514, 518, 520.

86. Jones v. United States 137 U.S. 202 (1890) at 212-13.

87. Poore op. cit. 1334. The Virginia senators had four year staggered terms, Ibid. 1910.

88. O'Donoghue v. United States 289 U.S. 516 (1933).

89. Williams v. United States 289 U.S. 553 (1933).

90. Montesquieu's L'Esprit des Lois may assume a similar distinction in the titles of Books XII and XI, that is "Liberty in Relation to the Subject" and "Liberty with Regard to the Constitution." The one concerns judicial and administrative processes while the other places final emphasis upon the tripartite legislature—at mid-point dismissing the judiciary as "in some measure next to nothing." XI, Ch. 6, par. 32. Also, a historian of constitutional theory says that "separation of powers" has nothing to do with "the independence of the judges." McIlwain op. cit. 141.

91. United States Constitution I, 6, par. 2.

92. Stephenson and Marcham op. cit. 612.

93. Lovell op. cit. 418-21.

94. "Walpole is usually considered the first Prime Minister . . . Yet in many ways Walpole and his immediate successors were quite different from their twentieth-century descendant." Lovell op. cit. 445.

95. Poore op. cit. 372.

96. Ordinances of the Convention, July 1775, IV, 8, 9. The Proceedings of the Convention of Delegates for the Counties and Corporations in the Colony of Virginia, 1775. Reprinted: Richmond: Ritchie, Trueheart and Du-val (1816) 47. (Copy in Newberry Library, Chicago.)

97. Poore op. cit. 1618, 1910.

98. Ibid. 1313 (mis-titled Constitution of 1844).

99. Ibid. 1545 (Pa.), 276 (Del.), 1413 (N.J.).

100. Ibid. 380 (Ga.) 819 (Md.).

101. Articles of Confederation, Art. V.

102. August 14, 1787; the provision was discussed also on June 22, 23, 26 and September 1, 14, 1787.

103. Congressional-administrative interrelationship in legislation is clearly evident in those statutes which leave much of their meaning to administrative regulations. Increasingly, Congress has reserved a "veto" by either house over such regulations. For an argument that this is unconstitutional, see Robert G. Dixon, Jr., "Congress, Shared Administration, and Executive Privilege" Harvey C. Mansfield, Sr. (Ed.) Congress Against the President New York: Praeger (1975) 125-40 at 126, 139. The opposition to the "veto" seems not to consider adequately the tentative character of the first congressional action. Final legislative judgment may not be feasible until the relevant committees have held hearings on the regulations as applied for a year or two.

THE WIDE SCOPE

OF MIXED POWER GOVERNMENT

The Constitution of the United States embodies a considerably more comprehensive pattern of authority distribution than the separate vesting of legislative, executive and judicial powers in three institutions. The main body of the Constitution includes scores of specific provisions. They set forth many particularized authorizations and numerous limitations as well as diverse procedures for the selection of officials. The total functional pattern indicates an underlying principle of complex interdependence more than threefold separation. For instance, the houses of Congress and the presidency have mixed roles in such important matters as considering the state of the Union, approving statutes, adopting treaties, controlling expenditures, appointing officials, and carrying powers into execution.

The common designation for this interrelated arrangement is "checks and balances." More precisely, it is "shared functions." Here, we will use the term "mixed power government" to stand for both concepts.

This chapter will explore the nature and scope of the mixed power pattern. It will examine checks and balances first as a distinct principle and then as related to separation of powers. Next we will discuss the concept of shared functions, and its application in representation, the control of administration, and the duty to cooperate. Finally we will seek to determine whether the division of the formal executive branch into separate presidential and administrative realms is compatible with the principles of checks and balances and shared functions.

The Alternative Doctrine of Checks and Balances

The meanings as well as the names of the constitutional doctrines of authority distribution often are confused or commingled. William Gwyn, in his scholarly study of separation of powers, makes a primary point of their distinct character. He criticizes those who attempt to justify separation of powers by explaining checks and balances. Professor Gwyn finds that "balance" is one of five arguments for the separation of powers, but he asserts that if the two doctrines are not distinguishable then there is little sense to James Madison's contention "in Federalist Nos. 48 and 51 that checks and balances are required to maintain a proper separation of powers."[1]   The other two foremost analysts of the origin and meaning of separation of powers, that is, Francis D. Wormuth and M.J.C. Vile, also consider that doctrine to be distinct, at least analytically, from other principles of constitutional arrangement, such as mixed government and checks and balances.[2]

The preceding chapter examined the one-to-one allocation of legislative, executive and judicial processes among three separate institutions apart from other patterns of distributed authority, including checks and balances.   In the same logical manner, this chapter will undertake to analyze that more complex pattern, not as so many exceptions to an idealized separate power theory, but as a distinct principle of constitutional allocation.   The objective is to ascertain whether checks and balances in itself encompasses—and thus adds legitimacy to—the existing separation of presidential and administrative forces within the formal executive branch.

We saw in the preceding chapter that three-branch-separate-function government has limited applicability.   The principle of checks and balances has more flexibility as well as more breadth.   This is the case from both institutional and functional viewpoints.   Checks and balances involves a more comprehensive recognition of an underlying precept of human psychology, that is, the need of checking political power with political power.[3]

A 1925 opinion of the Supreme Court examines the constitutional character of cross allocation—the assignment of a function of one general type to an institution of another general type.   The case involves the presidential power to grant reprieves and pardons.[4]   The Court rejects the contention that the possession of such a judge-like authority by the chief executive tends "to destroy the independence of the judiciary and violate the primary constitutional principle of a separation of the legislative, executive and judicial powers."[5]   The opinion of Chief Justice Taft points out that the Constitution does not keep the three powers entirely separate.   "Complete independence and separation between the three branches," the Court says, "are not attained, or intended, as other provisions of the Constitution and the normal operation of the government under it easily demonstrate."   Chief Justice Taft identifies other provisions which cut across the correspondence of three functions and three institutions.   He notes that "one House of Congress can withhold all appropriations and stop the operations of government" and that the Senate can "hold up all appointments."   He also calls attention to the veto power of the president and to the authority of the House and Senate through impeachment and trial to remove executive and judicial officers.[6]

Although separate powers and checks and balances often are commingled, they can be counter-principles.   They may serve competing interests in conflicts between the president and Congressional units.   The separation maxim may provide one side with a claim of constitutional propriety and the checks and balances principle do the same for the other side. The separate function model tends to favor the institution which seeks to act alone; that is most often the president. Thus, if the issue is whether Congress may require the president to obtain prior approval by relevant committees before sending military units outside the country, the separate power theory would tend to support the claim of the White House that such a limitation is unconstitutional whereas the checks and balances doctrine would favor the Capitol Hill position.[7] That would leave the final answer to the weighing of political and personal forces in the balance.

The course of the presidency during 1967-1974 brought a reappraisal of separate action by the chief executive and of the desirability of checks upon that office. Those who had favored presidential activism and executive unity saw that separate power could aid "imperialism" as well as "positivism." Erwin C. Hargrove explains, in respect of what he calls the "crisis of the contemporary Presidency," that "an energetic Presidency seems to be the key to policy and program achievement in our fragmented political systems, yet that same energy took us into Vietnam and was responsible for the crimes of Watergate."[8]

The two doctrines may appeal to different types of thinkers, such as idealists and pragmatists. The pure theory of separate power, with its simple trinity of corresponding functions and institutions, is a feature of our transcendent ideology. In contrast, the broad principle of checks and balances appeals to persons with empirical perspective and a sense of the actual uses of power. It also allows the basic formula of checking power with power to be applied against new types of concentration, such as those within the executive branch. Thus, checks and balances may provide wider assurance against abuses of authority than the three-branch-separate-function pattern.[9]

Institutionally, the center of checks and balances is in the Senate, and that may give mixed power distribution an impregnable position. Three function government does not require a senate. A representative assembly, a chief executive and a supreme court, can provide separate legislative, executive and judicial powers. But the senate, with its negative on enactment of statutes, on treaties and on superior appointments, has the keystone place in constitutionally prescribed checks and balances.[10] At the same time, it is the most protected institution in the United States government. The provision for amending the Constitution declares that "no state, without its consent, shall be deprived of its equal suffrage in the Senate." Thus, a single state could prevent the elimination of the Senate, or a change in the method of representation. But there is no restriction upon the changes which an ordinary amendment could make to the House of Representatives, the presidency, or the Supreme Court and other courts.

The Integration of Distribution Patterns

The Constitution of the United States, despite its formal facade of separate legislative, executive and judicial powers, promptly embraces the traditional pattern of mixed government. Article I, by authorizing presidential veto of measures approved by the two houses of Congress, establishes a tripartite process of statutory legislation.

The mechanism of interdependence by mutual negative among three politically counteracting forces is western history's most persistent paradigm of deconcentrated government.

The emergence of mixed government is a feature of classical thought. It involves a transition from simple to compound forms. The historian Herodotus distinguishes monarchy, aristocracy and democracy. Plato explains ideal and scientific patterns in his Republic and Statesman but his more final wisdom in the Laws is that there are two mother forms of government—monarchy and democracy. Every good government, he says, should include some of both in order to attain a moderation of both stability and freedom.[11] Such a combination is likely to give aristocracy a central position.

Aristotle in his Politics seems at first to come close to the modern doctrine of separate powers. He says that government consists of three types of authority: deliberative, executive and judicial. The first includes the enactment of laws but also the appointment of magistrates and other functions. Moreover, he does not assign each kind to a corresponding agency; rather he subdivides the three types and parcels out units to oligarchic and democratic forces with the aim of optimum balance. Moreover, he keeps coming back to the potential merits of an outstanding king.[12] Polybius and Cicero sum up the classical wisdom with their advocacy of the mixed rule of the one, the few and the many, or monarchy, aristocracy and democracy.[13]

Modern constitutional practice and theory dates from the Cromwellian Instrument of Government (1653) and James Harrington's ideal of "the senate proposing, the people resolving, and the magistracy executing."[14] John Locke probably is the father of modern doctrines of mixed power constitutionalism. His Second Treatise on Civil Government (1690) expounds at least three threefold models of distribution. First, there is a natural law trinity of making rules, judging and executing; then there is the division of governmental power into legislative, executive and "federative" (or external) functions; and finally there is the mutual sharing of legislative authority by three forces--a single hereditary person, an assembly of hereditary nobility and an assembly of representatives chosen by the people.[15] The Convention of 1787 at Philadelphia rejected hereditary office but otherwise worked all three designs into the United States Constitution.

Eighteenth century political thought gives more attention to the counteraction of political forces than to the separation of legal processes.

Viscount Bolingbroke, Baron Montesquieu, David Hume, William Blackstone and John Adams each advocate a three institution system of legislation. Bolingbroke attacks the exclusive assignment of legislative power, whether to the King, Lords, or Commons; he favors a "limited Monarchy," and a "division of power" which entails the sharing of authority among the three institutions. [16] David Hume says that "a hereditary prince, a nobility without vassals, and a people voting by their representatives form the best monarchy, aristocracy, and democracy." [17] Montesquieu, like Locke, has at least three sets of three powers—first, legislative, law of nations executive and civil law executive; then the familiar legislative, executive and judicial powers; and lastly "the fundamental constitution" composed of a popular assembly, a senate and the executivo. [18]

William Blackstone's Commentaries on the Laws of England (1765) says that "the true excellence of the English government" consists in the fact that "all the parts of it form a mutual check upon each other." In the legislature, "the people are a check upon the nobility, and the nobility a check upon the people; by the mutual privilege of rejecting what the other has resolved: while the king is a check upon both, which preserves the executive power from encroachments." [19] Blackstone adds that "this very executive is again checked, and kept within due bounds by the two houses, through the privilege they have of enquiring into, impeaching, and punishing the conduct . . . of his evil and pernicious counsellors." Blackstone compares the three institutions to "distinct powers in mechanics" which "jointly impel the machine of government in a direction different from what either, acting by themselves, would have done," but in "a direction which constitutes the true line of liberty and happiness of the community." [20] Blackstone's Commentaries became almost a bible for legal education, and probably was more widely read by the American constitution makers of 1776-89 than any other single volume. [21]

John Adams, whose writings on government are more comprehensive and more systematic than those of any other American of the founding period, emphasizes checks and balances. He strongly advocates a three power legislature of the one-few-and-many pattern. [22] He explains that a "single assembly" is apt to be avaricious and to grow ambitious, and that there is a necessity of "giving the executive power a negative upon the legislative." He sees dangers of these powers encroaching upon each other. To avoid that, "let a distinct assembly be constituted as a mediator between two extreme branches of the legislature, that which represents the people and that which is vested with the executive power." [23] These comments suggests that Adams viewed executive strength in relation to its veto, and that he considered the executive to be part of the legislature but not to be representative of the people. Adams may have been the author of the declaration in the Massachusetts Bill of Rights of 1780 that there should be separate exercise of legislative, executive and judicial powers "to the end it may be a government of laws and not of men." Thus, "a government of laws" means separate bodies of officials with interrelated functions.

The American constitution makers of the 1770s and the 1780s were aware of the potential benefits of checks and balances without recourse to either Montesquieu or Blackstone or other writers. Their colonial experience had taught them the value of a separate legislative assembly and an independent judiciary in checking or balancing the powers of the royal governors and the aristocratic councils. They readily adopted the three way distribution of superior political authority. The slightly revised constitution of Connecticut in 1776 said that it was a declaration of "the Governor, and Council, and House of Representatives, in General Court assembled."[24] The New Jersey constitution of the same year asserted that "the government of this Province shall be vested in a Governor, Legislative Council and General Assembly."[25] All except two of the other states had bicameral legislatures, and each of these—Georgia and Pennsylvania—had an executive council. The one in Georgia may have been like a senate but in Pennsylvania it was the head of the executive system. Pennsylvania did not have a single chief magistrate until 1789. Many state executives—Delaware and New Hampshire each used the title "President"—lacked veto power. The period 1776-89 is noted for weak governorships but in general the legislature power was divided between countervailing institutions.[26] Today, each state has a governor and, except for Nebraska, a bicameral legislature. State government embodies the principle of checks and balances in representation, legislation and execution.

The national constitutional convention of 1787 utilized the principle of mutual negative in several ways. The grand compromise, which set the large state dominance of the House of Representatives against the small state advantage in the Senate, is the prime example. The principle can be found in the convention design for the electoral college method of selecting presidents[27] and in the presidential-senatorial appointment of superior executive and judicial officials.

The Constitution gives superiority to the checks and balances principle also by establishing three mixed power systems of making law. In addition to the process of enacting statutes by the two houses of Congress and the presidency, there is the method of adopting treaties. Statutes and treaties have equal standing. In case of conflict, the latest controls. In fact, the Constitution may place treaties on a higher plane. It provides that the supreme law of the land includes laws made "in pursuance" of the Constitution, and treaties made under "the Authority of the United States." There is the possibility that treaty provisions need not be pursuant to the Constitution. Clearly, the procedure for treaties differs from that for statutes. For treaties, the House has no prescribed role and approval by the Senate requires two thirds vote of the members present. The president and the Senate in effect have absolute negatives upon each other. There is for treaties no equivalent to the override procedure by which the Congress can enact a statute over a presidential veto.

The third system of legislation concerns amendments to the Constitution. This entails proposal by two thirds vote of each house of Congress and ratification by the legislatures (or special conventions) of three fourths of the states. The Constitution prescribes no role for the president in the amending process but he may be involved politically. The roles of the Supreme Court in the various types of legislation range from bit part to stardom.

Thus, the four institutions have varying-participations in different areas of governmental activity. Even the number involved may change-- constitutional distribution is a flexible and often self-adjusting matter.

Several political science specialists indicate that checks and balances is the dominant principle. Arthur J. Holcombe's descriptive analysis of the American constitutional system asserts: "The American Whigs generally admired the British theory of separation of powers with its practical embodiment in a system of checks and balances."[20] Charles W. Dunn, in a 1975 commentary on the presidency, says that the Constitution "establishes not so much a doctrine of separation of powers as a fusion of powers."[29] Each of two scholarly studies of conflict process consider the two doctrines to be implicit corollaries, and, jointly, to place deliberation before action.[30] We will have more to say on this last matter in the section on the shared duty to cooperate.

Many general political science explanations of the American national government tend to treat separation as preliminary to checks and balances.[31] One such analysis states that the 1787 "convention delegates felt that separation of powers in itself was not sufficient to prevent tyranny." Another asserts that the Framers "felt that despotic or arbitrary government could be prevented only through a system of *checks and balances* by which each branch possessed the ability to curtail excessive power by either of the other two.[32] In fact, one general explanation declares that "the separation of powers is without purpose unless it results in checks and balances."[33] Still more incisive is an assertion that frankly subordinates the three-branch doctrine. "The key to the constitutional system," it says, "is not the principle of separation of powers but the principle of checks and balances."[34] The dominance of the mixed power principle over the separate function model facilitates the recognition of the legitimacy of two counteracting branches engaged in executive/administrative functions.

The Integrating Formula of Shared Functions

The foremost development during the past quarter century in the political science explanation of the interplay of the two doctrines of constitutional distribution has been the increasing acceptance of the principle of "separated institutions *sharing* powers." Richard Neustadt, one-time aide to President Truman and now a Harvard professor, is the recognized initiator of the formula. He contends that it describes the constitutional system more accurately than "separation of powers."[35] The formula can serve to integrate the different theories of allocation. We will also consider whether it characterizes the relationship of the presidential and administrative realms of the formal executive branch.

Nearly half of the more than fifty political science explanations of the national government for university students approve expressly in some degree the integrating principle of shared powers. Some make the formula "an essential ingredient of the separation of powers." Others deem it superior to the more traditional doctrine. For instance, one asserts that although "the phrase 'separation of powers' has a measure of accuracy," it is "in many respects a most misleading" description. "It is more accurate to say that the American Constitution, through a system of 'checks and balances' provides for a government of separated institutions sharing powers." [36] Another says that "the concept of 'separation of powers' is really misnamed, for what we are really talking about is a sharing, not a separating of power." [37] The Neustadt formula, in effect, limits separation to institutions and associates functions with sharing. Yet we need further analysis of the ways in which institutions share functions.

Political science explanations rarely differentiate between the two general types of sharing functions. In one kind, two or more institutions perform the same kind of action on a mutual negative basis, such as the two houses of Congress voting separately to approve proposed legislation before it is presented to the president for his approval or rejection. There is historical support for the proposition that the separation of institutions is preliminary to at least this type of sharing. James Wilson pointed out at the Constitutional Convention on July 21, 1787 that:

> The separation of the departments does not require that they should have separate objects but that they should act separately though on the same objects. It is necessary that the two branches of the Legislature should be separate and distinct, yet they are both to act precisely on the same object.

This, of course, is not the same as vesting legislative, executive and judicial functions in separate institutions. That involves the second type of sharing. The amending process is an example of the first type because both Congress and the state legislatures must approve the same particular proposal. The federal division of law making authority between the states and the national government is not strictly the sharing of functions because action by both is not required for any particular statutory enactment.

The other type of sharing involves actions which are different in particular but interdependent in general. The foremost example is the trio of action types necessary for criminal punishment, that is, enacting penal laws, executing them, and making judicial determinations. Other examples are the establishment of offices by Congress and the appointments by the president or a department head; and the appropriation of money by Congress and its withdrawal from the Treasury. Judicial review of legislative, executive, administrative, or lower court action, is also the second type because appellate review differs from the primary action. The functions of the separate administrative branch involve this second type of sharing insofar as the particular actions differ from the related activities of Congress, the presidency or the courts.

Political science explanations of governmental behavior during the past quarter century often have extended the general notion of shared functions to the point of assigning all institutions a common function, such as making decisions, converting inputs into outputs, or delivering policy.[38] Frequently, the consequence of such an approach is the treatment of the presidency, the Congress, the courts and the administrative bureaucracy to be four types of distinguishable "political subsystems," each engaged in making policy. That tends to obliterate the traditional contrast of functions expressed in the usual statements of the separate power doctrine. "In the realities of the policymaking process," one analysis says, "there is little in the way of separation." More specifically, it explains: "The emergence of subsystems has served to bridge whatever gap was intended to exist between branches, as interest groups, executive agencies, and congressional subcommittees all operate in a particular policy area serving their specialized constituencies."[39] Analyses which stress this type of approach to the operation of the national government naturally give less or lower scale attention to the express constitutional functions.

Separate powers without the duty of sharing functions may serve less to avoid tyranny of action than to assure political confrontation between a president and Congress. One political science volume asserts that "separation of powers has meant struggle for power" and that "both the legislative and executive branches have devised numerous strategies not mentioned in the Constitution."[40] The separate function doctrine may support unproductive combat between Congress and the president, particularly but not exclusively when different parties hold the Capitol and the White House. Harry Truman was a striking example but Presidents Kennedy, Johnson, Nixon, Ford and Carter, also had their problems. Congress, in its turn, may blame the White House for almost anything. Sometimes quiet accommodation follows conspicuous confrontation but the principle of separation serves the politics of antagonism.

The negative potential of the separation pattern was its original *raison d'etre*. The distribution of governing authority among politically opposing institutions was deliberately designed to frustrate governmental activists. It developed during the seventeenth and eighteenth centuries in the republican and revolutionary challenges to monarchical despotism. It was extended from time to time as middle or upper class protection against a "tyranny of the majority" danger in popularly elected assemblies. At 1776-89, restraint of government was likely to be on the side of individual liberty as then understood to mean freedom from interference.[41] Now, the meaning of liberty is more "positive," stressing the freedom to develop one's capacity in conditions of comparative equality. Government in this century has a larger proportion of direct benefits, and there is a greater expectation of affirmative actions. Many persons ask it to provide positive ideological and symbolic satisfactions. The 1967-76 antagonism to government probably is an interlude in the several decades of rising expectations, more group benefits, and welfare liberalism. Yet, in face of the call for more governmental activity, there is still unreconciled devotion to the doctrines of separation and checks and balances and their use to hinder action. In part, this may derive from an assumption that the only alternative is simple dictatorship, either by an executive or legislative, or perhaps a judicial body. Also, there may be insufficient recognition that there are now additional restraining forces, such as the competition of the major parties, both internally and externally. Together, these factors may cause "divided government," that is, a Congress of one party and a White House of the other. This happened during sixteen of the thirty years, 1946-76.[42]

A number of political science explanations of American national government point out the negative potential of the separate power doctrine and its corollary. For instance, one asks: "Has the separation of powers, with its system of checks and balances, worked not only to prevent tyranny but also to prevent the effective operation of government?"[43] Another makes a more general observation: "Many political scientists dislike the principle of separation of powers because checks and balances lead to considerable inefficiency."[44]

The Shared Power of Representation

Analyses of authority distribution commonly do not consider the function of electoral representation. Yet, from the viewpoint of republican and democratic legitimacy, that power is more fundamental than legislation, execution or adjudication.   The elected institutions are directly responsible and responsive to the active voters of the nation. The two houses of Congress and the presidency comprise the foremost pattern of separate institutions sharing powers. Their distinctive identities have deep political roots; they derive from differences in the constituencies, in the frequency of elections, and in the contrasting numbers of members. The presidency has no official role in the amending process, but that office and one or both houses of Congress share most other superior functions.   These include representation, legislation, appropriation, appointment of high officials, review of administration and public criticism of governmental operations.

The modern presidency emphasizes the role of chief representative considerably more than that of chief administrator. Since about 1840, presidents have claimed that they represent the entire nation, or all the people, while a senator or representative is the voice of only a state or a district. A more accurate comparison might be between the presidency and the two houses as entities in themselves but voters and journalistic commentators look to individual human personalities. Even so, the president may be primarily responsive to a particular segment of the national society, such as the urban voters in large cities. In fact, there may be effective representation of the entire nation only through the combined force of the House, the Senate and the presidency, and perhaps, not even then.

The political pattern of three institutions sharing the function of representation brings the competitive allocation of high authority to the reach of the citizens themselves. Each voter has the potential of participating in the control of different types of officials. Active competition among multiple channels of public representation is esteemed by most political scientists today as it was by most delegations at the 1787 Constitutional Convention. In fact, enlightened social analysts at many stages of western history have revered the idea of separate channels of communication between the political elements of the society and the decision making offices of the respective governments. Classical philosophers as well as modern social scientists favored the recognition of the different economic or cultural forces among the society.[45] Today many political analysts consider the openness of the input gateways to be one of the principal tests of legitimacy.[46] We may find support for this view not merely in Madison's theory of countervailing factions but even more fundamentally in the attention which the 1787 Convention gave to the original system of mixed representation. The delegates spent much time and effort on questions of how far the different forces of the nation should be able to control the House, the Senate and the presidency.

The constitutional pattern of three elected institutions reflects the classical theory of mixed government. In fact, there is a stronger contrast of monocratic, aristocratic and democratic forces in the American national government today than there was in classical Athens and Rome. Our political system has a broader base—they excluded non-natives, slaves and women as well as minors. Ours also has a higher pinnacle than either of those two. That suggests that our methods of distributing authority derive more from our own experiences than from the theories of other lands in previous eras.

The American state constitutions of the independence period gave both ideological and practical priority to the function of electoral representation. They made the elected assemblies more appropriate for the general functions of representation than for the specific tasks of legislation. The state declarations of rights in 1776 relied less upon natural rights and the theory of revolution than upon the frequency of elections to keep the governments responsive to the tax paying public.[47] Nearly all of the states specified one year terms for legislators. Even the two year term prescribed subsequently for national representatives leaves little respite between elections. National as well as state legislators must be continuously involved in communication with their constituencies in order to ascertain and appraise the feedback from official actions as well as the changing pattern of input supports and demands.[48]

The attachment of the American constitution makers to the idea of mixed representation is evident in the readiness of the new states to establish second legislative chambers. Senates were not required by the doctrine of separate legislative, executive and judicial powers. Moreover, the historical precedents were not attractive. The Roman senate had been oligarchic, the House of Lords was still largely hereditary, and the colonial councils often had been agents of the governors in exerting pressure upon the representative assemblies and even upon the courts. Yet the state governments incorporated second chambers or councils from the start. Among the new constitutions of 1776-84, all but two prescribed upper houses and those authorized executive councils.[49]

The element of tripartite representation that most restrains policy innovation is the contrasting political attitudes of the institutions. That was the aim of the 1787 Convention in establishing bicameralism and in authorizing a presidential veto. The Convention, in line with eighteenth century observation generally, saw each house of Congress as a monolithic expression of a particular socio-economic position. The delegates sought to assure the countervailing force of the pattern by prescribing a distinct method of selecting each house. "The people" chose directly only the lower house. At the time, "the people" were the property owners, mostly family farmers, because of the qualifications for voting. But the nationalist supporters of the Convention believed that even that limited amount of "democracy" needed institutional restraint. Governor Randolph declared that a check upon the more popular branch was necessary because the prevailing evils burdening the country originated in "the turbulence and follies of democracy." James Madison asserted that the senate would proceed "with more coolness, with more system, and with more wisdom than the popular branch." He wanted a small membership because the larger the number "the more they partook of the infirmities of their constituencies."[50]

The Convention delegates assumed that the two houses would represent different socio-economic forces. The identity of the two groups appears in the arguments of a Massachusetts delegate against the direct election of the second chamber. There are, Elbridge Gerry explained, "two great interests, the landed interest and the commercial including the stockholders." Drawing both branches from the people, he argued "will leave no security to the latter interest," while the selection of the senators by the state legislatures "will be most likely to provide some check in favor of the commercial interests against the landed."[51] Hugh Williamson of North Carolina summarized the arguments for mixed republicanism: "The different modes of representation in the different branches will serve as a mutual check."[52] This shows again that the Convention was motivated more by the practical devices of political checks and balances than by the legalistic theory of three separate types of processes.

Anti-democratic views appear also in the comments on the difference in the terms of the members of the two houses of Congress. Governor Randolph sharply defended the longer tenure for senators. "The democratic licentiousness of the State Legislatures" shows the need of a "firm Senate" to control "the democratic branch of the National Legislature," he asserted. A Senate may be needed also, he added, to guard against "encroachments of the Executive who will be apt to form combinations with the demagogues of the popular branch." At that time the majority of the delegations had approved congressional selection of the president without deciding whether the two houses would vote separately or as a joint body. James Madison, who repeatedly expressed his fear of a radical representative assembly, stated in this debate that long terms would aid stability; otherwise "the popular branch would still be too great an overmatch" for the -senate.[53] Thus, the 1787 Convention found the necessity of an upper house in its countervailing political power.

There may be a similar reason behind the grant of a modified veto to the president and the requirement of a two-thirds vote to override. The presidential veto is not limited to matters which have a direct adverse bearing upon the executive function of applying the law. It may be used to negative legislation because of its quality as law or policy in general. It is a principal factor in the rise of the presidency as "chief legislator" and the full development of a tripartite legislative process. The veto also strengthens the argument of presidents that they can speak for the whole nation.

The full force of tripartite representation came with the presidency of Andrew Jackson. Whereas the Virginia dynasty of Jefferson, Madison and Monroe had sought, and at times with success, to attain political integration of the legislative and executive leaderships, President Jackson undertook to challenge and even to overpower the houses of Congress. He gave new force to the use of the separate channels of representation in the development of confrontation and public political drama.

Next, we will consider the potentials of the tripartite arrangement for broadening the responsiveness and the responsibility of the administrative units.

The Shared Control of Administration

The Constitution specifically authorizes Congress to establish "post offices and post roads," "to raise and support armies," and "to provide and maintain a navy." But mostly the power of Congress to establish executive institutions derives from a broadly worded provision. It is the eighteenth enumerated power:[54]

To make all laws which shall be necessary and proper for carrying into execution, the foregoing powers, and all other Powers vested by this Constitution in the Government of the United States, or in any Department or Officer thereof.

This permits Congress to carry into execution, not only the express grants to it, but also the powers assigned to any department or officer. Thus, Congress has authority to provide for carrying into execution the constitutional powers of the president. Professor Peter Woll explicates the primacy of Congress in this matter. He points out that the "organic power" to create and abolish agencies "is entirely contained in Congress," and that there is no way in which this authority can be inferred from Article II, that is, the presidential article. If presidents have established some agencies, Professor Woll points out that "this has been under a grant of delegated power from Congress." Accordingly, he adds, "the bureaucracy is always an agent of Congress," unless the legislature chooses to set up different arrangements. Congress may decide to make agencies responsible to the president, but, he concludes, "it is a common mistake to assume that the bureaucracy is 'the executive branch' and entirely accountable to the White House."[55]

The necessary and proper clause is one of three constitutional provisions which refer expressly to departments. Each of the others assumes rather than authorizes their existence. The Confederation Congress had established three departments in 1781 and they were functioning while the Convention of 1787 met.[56] It evidently expected that they would continue.

The second provision referring to departments appears to permit an exception to a general pattern of relationships. It says that the president may "require the Opinion in writing of the principal Officer in each of the executive Departments, upon any subject relating to the duties of their respective Offices."[57] That seems to assume that the principal officers or department heads were not and would not be simply the president's men. Why stipulate that he has a right to their opinions in writing if they are to be solely or even primarily responsible to him? If the aim was to clarify or emphasize there were several matters of more importance, such as the authority to issue orders or decrees, which the constitution does not specify. Thus, the provision suggests that the department heads are primarily responsible to institutions other than the president; obviously they would be the houses of Congress, as they were under the then existing Articles of Confederation.

The third constitutional reference to departments appears in the clause that "Congress may by Law vest the Appointment of such inferior Offices, as they think proper, in the President alone, in the Courts of Law or in the Heads of Departments."[58] Hence, Congress may confer appointive power directly upon the principal officer of a department rather than give the authority to the president and allow him in his discretion to authorize the department head. This last is now the legal procedure often used but is a matter of statutory discretion rather than constitutional need.

The third of these clauses, like the others, suggests that the Convention assumed that there would be direct relations between the houses of

Congress and the departments. This concerns not only establishment, authorizations and appropriations, but also the review or surveillance of operations. There is further support for this proposition in the constitutional requirement of senatorial approval of high level appointments, such as departmental secretaries. The executive power only shares in such appointments. In fact, the character of the authority to appoint officials seems not to be an intrinsically determinable matter. For instance, the states at one time or another have used at least three methods of selecting judges. At the start the legislatures often selected them, and now in some states the governors appoint them while in others the voters elect judges. Thus, the power is legislative, executive or electoral as the case may be.

Moreover, the power to appoint may not carry with it a power to remove. A president may not remove the judges whom he appoints and the Supreme Court has extended that principle to the quasi-judicial officials of administrative regulatory commissions.[59] Congress may not restrict the president's authority to remove certain top executive officials but it has severely limited or prohibited his right to remove most government employees. Where he cannot remove he may have difficulty exercising control. These are some of the various matters which indicate that the administrative system is not merely the arms and legs of the presidency, but has the autonomy which comes from being accountable to more than one institution.

A number of leading analysts of the national executive support, designedly or otherwise, the logical implicaton of these three constitutional clauses that the department heads are as much responsible to the House and the Senate as to the president. Professor Erwin C. Hargrove gives this explanation: [60]

> The President is not made master in his own Executive house by the Constitution. The constitutional structure of separate institutions sharing powers gives Congress the authority to establish ˋExecutive departments and thereby to attempt to control them through the process of making appropriations and writing statutes.

Another political science specialist, Rowland Egger, states that while the president derives some authority from the Constitution, the powers of heads of departments and agencies are "wholly statutory." Dorothy James observes that the rivalry between the president and Congress for the control of the "bureaucracy" has allowed it to "become an independent power in its own right." Louis W. Koenig sees dual supervision. "The executive branch has not one but two managers--the President and his rival, Congress. Nearly everything the President does Congress can do, sometimes with greater effect." Peter Woll and Rochelle Jones are even more pointed: "The authority of 'chief administrator' is shared between the President and Congress."[61]

In summation, the three elected institutions--the House, the Senate and the presidency--while differing in many aspects, share not only the duties of representation and the rights of statutory legislation but also the responsibilities of directing the executive/administrative decision makers. In fact, they form a common class in contradistinction to the appointed executive officials, particularly the career policy makers. Cooperation among the three elected institutions, and a common effort in relation to the administrative units, may be more important in the operation of checks and balances, than counteraction among themselves.

The Shared Duty to Cooperate

Modern expectations give rise to another problem in the constitutional distribution of powers and limitations. This is whether the doctrines of separation and checks and balances are merely restrictive in their objectives or whether they may have positive potentials. In approaching this problem, we may first recognize that there are some situations in which the respective institutions need not share powers, others in which they might if they wish, and still others in which they must share. The Constitution leaves many uncertainties. For instance, it first indicates that legislation is for the houses of Congress but it soon gives the president substantial participation, such as the right to veto.

The Supreme Court has made a number of attempts at identifying what functions may or may not be shared. The first effort probably was that by Chief Justice Marshall in 1825 when he declared that Congress could not delegate what is "strictly and exclusively legislative."[62] Presumably that is still valid. As an abstract idea, it preserves the ideal of functionally exclusive institutions without interfering with the massive delegation of legislative-like authority by Congress.

The last major attempt of the Supreme Court to deal with the law on the sharing of functions appears to be the executive privilege case of 1974. There, President Nixon claimed that the separate power doctrine justified his refusal to share information with the judiciary even on a criminal trial subpoena. He not only claimed "executive privilege" from disclosure, but also contended that the separation of powers doctrine precludes the judicial review of a president's claim of privilege. On this point Chief Justice Burger stated that the judicial power vested in the federal courts "can no more be shared with the Executive Branch than the Chief Executive, for example, can share with the Judiciary the veto power, or the Congress share with the Judiciary the power to override a Presidential veto." Any other conclusion, the Chief Justice asserted, "would be contrary to the basic concept of separation of powers and the checks and balances that flow from the scheme of a tripartite government."[63] We may note in passing that the court combines the two doctrines. The holding of the court means that the executive may need to share with the judiciary--and sooner or later with the public--the record of internal communications that were undertaken in pursuit of executive functions for executive purposes.

More enlightening on the immediate point are the examples of powers which need not, and perhaps cannot be shared--the veto power and the power to override. These are specific procedures and they suggest a rather technical approach to the identification of exclusiveness. In fact, they indicate a sharing in the larger process of making law. The Supreme Court cannot veto legislation but it can hold acts of Congress contrary to the Constitution and thus in part have a similar effect. In substance, the houses of Congress, the presidency, the Supreme Court, and the administrative branch each have some degree of legislative negative upon each other. There is considerable sharing of the law making function even when there is no sharing of particular procedures. Again, we need to go beyond the simple separation of legislative, executive and judicial powers to ascertain the effective pattern of constitutional distribution.

The Supreme Court seems to have supported this proposition. It said that a president has some privilege to withhold confidential conversations and correspondence. "The privilege is fundamental to the operation of government and inextricably rooted in the separation of powers under the Constitution," Chief Justice Burger stated for the Court.[64] Thus, one basis of the privilege is the operation of government generally. Likewise, the Court indicated that other branches of the United States government, expressly the judicial system, have a similar claim to confidentiality of deliberations. Hence, "executive privilege" may use the term "executive" in this meaning of "secret" rather than something exclusive to the executive branch.

Still more to the point, the Court held that the presidential privilege is not absolute. Its strength is apt to depend upon the circumstances. It is strong when it concerns military or diplomatic secrets, and weaker when the demands are for use in a criminal prosecution. The more fundamental matter seems to be the standards for determining these rules of accommodation. The Court did not identify the criteria but it was definite that "the independence of the Executive Branch within its own sphere" is a limited matter. The Court asserted that "neither the doctrine of separation of powers, nor the need for confidentiality of high-level communications, without more, can sustain an absolute, unqualified Presidential privilege of immunity from judicial process under all circumstances."[65] Thus, we see again that the more determinative answer is in the doctrine of checks and balances rather than merely in the separation of powers itself. Moreover, the Court indicated that when both the judicial system and the executive are involved in a controversy, the Supreme Court rather than the president has the final say on the legal issue.

While the Court gave few indications of the precise limitations upon the separation doctrine, it did suggest that it is a matter of pragmatic and circumspect judgment rather than logical deduction. "The President's need for complete candor and objectivity from advisers calls for great deference from the courts," the Court stated. However, when "sensitive national security secrets" are not involved the duty "to do justice in criminal prosecutions" limits the presidential privilege.[66]

The Court turned next to the objective of the distribution pattern. It stated that "the Framers of the Constitution sought to provide a comprehensive system, but the separate powers were not intended to operate with absolute independence." Chief Justice Burger then quotes from the concurring opinion of the late Justice Jackson in the steel seizure case:[67]

> While the Constitution diffuses power the better to secure liberty, it also contemplates that practice will integrate the dispersed powers into a workable government. It enjoins upon its branches separateness but interdependence, autonomy but reciprocity.

This last suggests a common duty to cooperate toward the end of a "workable government." Montesquieu touched upon this type of problem. After stating that "the fundamental constitution" consists of a three part legislature, he said that the powers "naturally form a state of repose or inaction." Then he identified a basic counter force—"as there is a necessity for movement in the course of human affairs, they are forced to move, but still in concert."[68] The objective of constitutional distribution of authority may be not inaction but action in concert. The concept of separate institutions sharing powers would seem to be substantially more conducive to a cooperative attitude among congressional, presidential and administrative branches than the separate function concept.

A few of the political scientists engaged in explaining the American national government express displeasure with the negative tendencies of the separation of powers. Here, they may be more normative than descriptive but it is a logical consequence of the liberal activist conception of modern politics. "The great task of American government," one analyst states, "is to get these separate institutions to work together with some measure of effectiveness."[69] The more difficult process of seeking agreement among separate and often politically counteracting institutions, may result in a more widely acceptable end product. Two leading political scientists explain that the balances established in the Constitution required that the various units of government cooperate with one another to reach common objectives.[70]

Checks and Balances Within the Executive Branch

We have seen repeatedly that checks and balances is a more fundamental principle of constitutional distribution than separate legislative, executive and judicial powers. The foremost instances of check and balance within the official structure of the national government concern the three elected institutions—the House, the Senate and the presidency—with respect to representation, legislation and the guidance of the administrative branch.

The president and members of Congress encounter many difficulties in trying to direct the appointed officialdom. The come-and-go forces at the White House have an added problem with the career executives. Then the rivalry between Congress and the presidency aids administrative independence. Professor Neustadt points out that the "bureaucracy" serves more than one master. "A product of the separation between Congress and the presidency has been a separation of officialdom from both. The government departments," he explains, "are dependent upon both, subject in part to both, hence wholly subordinate to neither." [71]

Congress, under its constitutional authority to enact laws necessary and proper for carrying into execution the powers of the government, the departments and the officers, has implanted many types of checks and balances within the executive/administrative arrangement. Basically and broadly, the Congress has placed the large majority of specialized decision makers under merit system methods of appointment. This tends to protect them from the alternating partisanism of the White House. The distinction between noncareer and career administrators corresponds in substantial degree to the difference, articulated by Professors Schlesinger and Hargrove, between "presidential" and "permanent" government. [72] The forces which causes these two realms to check and balance each other have deep roots, legally, politically and ideologically. On the one side, there is short tenure with high status, and, on the other, career status with middle level position. Alternating general policy struggles against continuing specific rules. Ideologically, attentive publics revere the sovereign personality of a president but equally abhor any "spoils" system of selecting most government decision makers. The foundations of the presidential-administrative differentiation are perdurable. Realistically, we need to accept the division and try to comprehend its character and consequences.

Political scientists have explained that counteraction among operating units is the result of many factors. Bertram M. Gross in 1953 said that "there are more checks and balances within the executive branch itself than the Founding Fathers ever dreamed of when they wrote the Constitution." [73] One is the sense of career professionalism among specialized administrators. Grant McConnell said in both 1967 and 1976 that among "a whole series of obstacles to presidential influence" in the "federal bureaucracy," the chief is "inertia, a tendency to go on doing what has always been done." [74] But inertia is not mere inaction; it is a constant rate of motion. In extreme, .it might be resistance to any change; but it can result from a firm regard for consistency and the rule of law. Without the stability of uniform action, most of the time, the government would not operate in a tolerable manner. In our affairs, we need to be able to count upon a strong measure of consistency and predictability. There also must be a continuing force to carry the government through periods of presidential change or crisis. Philippa Strum touches upon this in her analysis of the presidency. "It is the greatest achievement of the American bureaucratic system that it continues to function no matter what happens on the electoral scene," [75] Professor Cronin adds another point. He states that the main complaint of the Kennedy-Johnson and the Nixon-Ford regimes was "the inertia of the bureaucracy" but White House aides, he points out, "repeatedly failed to understand the virtues of the bureaucracy, the experience and wisdom that lay behind its warnings and reluctance."[76]

The continuity and inertia of the career administrators often are in sharp contrast to the alternating partisanship of the presidency, and particularly to the attitude of a newly elected chief executive who promised to change governmental methods. Career executives may be partisans privately, and that may affect, intentionally or otherwise, their official decisions.[77]   But by and large their partisanship is noticeably less than that of the White House. Presidents are inherently partisan and they are apt to view "bureaucrats" to be either pro or con. When career officials try to be neutral, the White House may consider them to be part of the opposition. Some presidents assume that their election authorizes them to impose their own views upon the whole executive branch. Professors Woll and Jones, in April 1974, admonished at least the then president on this matter:[78]

> The President must respect the professionalism of a large part of the bureaucracy and not attempt to run it along partisan lines . . . . The bureaucracy must be able to carry on intact from one president to another . . . . While recognizing the importance of continuous checks upon bureaucratic power, a respect for the integrity and independence of the bureaucracy will enable it to meet the enormous responsibilities that have been thrust upon it.

The assertions of these political scientists that there is appreciable merit in the continuity and even in the inertia of the career administrators indicate the substantiality of the conflict between the continuing and the presidential governments. The enduring division within the executive system may be a substantial contribution to the purposes of the constitutional principle of checks and balances.

The unsystematic separation of executive officials into noncareer presidential and career administrative forces corresponds roughly to a division within each house of Congress. This is between the central party leaderships and the particularized interests among the subcommittees and the unofficial blocs that respond to the demands and supports of particular constituencies. Professor Rexford G. Tugwell, one of Franklin Roosevelt's "brain trust," stated in 1974 that the relations of appointed officials "with interested legislators are closer than any they have with the president."[79] The interactions between administrators and legislators may form a multiplicity of unofficial alliances. The centrifugal forces reflect a high degree of political as well as professional particularization. Professor McConnell finds this a key aspect of presidential-administrative relationships:[80]

> . . . it is questionable whether the presidency has kept up with the centrifugal tendency of the government. Many parts of the government have a large degree of autonomy within the

bureaucratic structure . . . . the bureaus and agencies of the federal government often have their own political sources of support and can act independently of presidential wishes.

Thus, specialization may be a principal reason for three significant developments: the vast aggregate of power held by the countless subunits of administration; the deepening chasm between the presidential executive forces and the career administrators; and the supporting relationships of the administrative and congressional subunits. Accordingly, the next chapter will consider from various angles the legitimizing aspects of specialization in our socio-political system.[81]

NOTES

1. William Gwyn The Meaning of Separation of Powers New Orleans: Tulane University Press (1967), 3, see also 26, 47, 48, 55, and 111. The other four arguments for the separation of powers are the rule of law, accountability, efficiency and common interest.

2. Francis D. Wormuth The Origins of Modern Constitutionalism New York: Harper and Bros. (1949) tends to associate separation of powers with governmental functions (59) and checks and balances with political forces or institutions (174), but such a difference may be a matter of approach. Mixed government usually refers to some pattern of the one, the few and the many. M.J.C. Vile Constitutionalism and the Separation of Powers Oxford: Clarendon Press (1967) suggests that separation of powers, despite its relation to the older theories of mixed and balanced government, emerged when a system based upon a mixture of King, Lords and Commons, seemed to be no longer relevant (3).

3. ". . . constant experience shows us that every man invested with power is apt to abuse it, . . . To prevent this abuse, it is necessary from the very nature of things that power should be a check to power." Montesquieu The Spirit of the Laws, XI, 4.

4. Ex parte Grossman 267 U.S. 87 (1925).

5. Ibid. at 119.

6. Ibid. at 119, 120.

7. "The spirit of administrative centralization implicit in the constitutional powers of the Presidency is effectively nullified by a second major feature of the Constitution—the concept of checks and balances . . . if the separation of powers doctrine tends to make clear and precise distinctions, . . . the concept of checks and balances tends to blur that distinction, . . . Louis C. Gawthrop Administrative Politics and Social Change New York: St. Martin's (1971) 21.

8. Erwin C. Hargrove The Power of the Modern Presidency Philadelphia: Temple University Press (1974) 3-4. Similarly: "The imperial presidency has developed because of the separation of the executive from Congress, and the establishment of independent prerogative powers in the presidency under the Constitution." Peter Woll Public Policy Cambridge, Mass.: Winthrop (1974) 120-21.

9. The two doctrines are "mutually contradictory" despite similar ends; one makes for "division and independence, the other interaction and

dependence," Louis W. Koenig The Chief Executive Third Edition, New York: Harcourt Brace Jovanovich (1975) 27.

10. "The development of a cabinet composed of department heads was both a cause and a result of the failure of the Senate to function effectively as an advisory body." Alfred H. Kelly and Winfred A. Harbison The American Constitution: Its Origins and Development Fourth Edition New York: W.W.-Norton (1970) 185.

11. Plato Laws 693, 756-57.

12. Aristotle, Politics III, 1x, 1280a; III, xv, 1286a, 1288a; IV, xiv-xvi; V, x, 1310b.

13. Kurt von Fritz, The Theory of the Mixed Constitution in Antiquity: A Critical Analysis of Polybius's Political Ideas New York: Columbia University Press (1954) 306. ". . . the best constituted state is one which is formed by the due combination of the three simple types, monarchy, aristocracy and democracy." Cicero On the Commonwealth, II, 23.

14. Charles Blitzer (Ed.) The Political Writings of James Harrington New York: Liberal Arts Press (1955) 61-78.

15. John Locke The Second Treatise of Civil Government IX, XII, XIX (par. 213).

16. Vile op. cit. 73.

17. David Hume "That Politics May Be Reduced to a Science" Charles W. Hendel (Ed.) David Hume's Political Essays Indianapolis: Bobbs-Merrill (1953) 12-23 at 15.

18. Montesquieu, op. cit. X, 6 par. 55. The Spirit of the Laws by Baron de Montesquieu New York: Hafner Publishing (1949) 160. The common academic belief that Montesquieu and in turn Blackstone and Delolme misinterpreted the British constitution has been challenged, Charles Morgan The Liberty of Thought and the Separation of Powers: Zaharoff Lecture for 1948 Oxford University Press (1948) 18, and John Plamanetz Man and Society New York: McGraw-Hill (1963) I, 181-94; discussed in Henry J. Merry Montesquieu's System of Natural Government Lafayette, Ind.; Purdue University Studies (1970) 299-303.

19. William Blackstone Commentaries on the Laws of England Oxford: Clarendon Press (1765) I, 150-51.

20. Ibid. 151.

21. Opinions differ on the influence of Montesquieu in America. See Paul M. Spurlin Montesquieu in America Baton Rouge: Louisiana State University Press (1940) and Benjamin F. Wright "Origins of the Separation of Powers in America," 13 Economica (1933) 169-85.

22. George A. Peek, Jr., The Political Writings of John Adams New York: Liberal Arts Press (1954) xix.

23. Ibid. 87, 88.

24. Benjamin Perley Poore (Ed.) The Federal and State Constitutions, Colonial Charters, and other Organic Laws of the United States Washington, D.C. Government Printing Office (1877) 257.

25. Ibid. 1311 (mis-titled Constitution of 1844).

26. Ibid. 377-83 (Ga), 821-27 (Md.), 960-69 (Mass.), 1283-91 (N.H.), 1311-13 (N.J.), 1332-37 (N.Y.), 1411-13 (N.C.), 1542-47 (Pa.), 1617-25 (S.C.), 1910-12 (Va.), and 273-78 (Del.).

27. The Convention gave control of the two stages of the process to the state legislatures and the House of Representatives.

28. Arthur N. Holcombe The Constitutional System Chicago: Scott, Foresman (1964) 29.

29. Charles W. Dunn The Future of the American Presidency Morristown, N.J.: General Learning (1975) 9.

30. The founders "provided mechanisms by which various branches could check and veto the activities of each other." Paul H. Conn Conflict and Decision Making: An Introduction to Political Science New York: Harper and Row (1971) 218; "Separation of powers and checks and balances can be quite unworkable." Dan Nimmo and Thomas D. Ungs American Political Patterns: Conflict and Consensus Third Edition Boston: Little, Brown (1973) 93.

31. One text says that "powers" are more accurately "processes" and that by participating in one another's processes "the three brances are in a position to *check and balance* one another's influence and political power." Richard A. Watson Promise and Performance in American Democracy Second Edition New York: John Wiley (1975) 45-46.

32. Dennis J. Palumbo American Politics New York: Appleton-Century-Crofts (1973) 48; Peter Woll and Robert Binstock America's Political System Second Edition New York: Random House (1975) 88.

33. Martin Dirnbach American Political Life: An Introduction to United States Government Homewood, Ill.: Dorsey (1071) 156.

34. John C. Livingston and Robert G. Thompson The Consent of the Governed Third Edition New York: Macmillan (1971) 159.

35. Richard E. Neustadt Presidential Power: The Politics of Leadership New York: John Wiley (1960, 1964) 33; (1976) 101.

36. William Ebenstein, C. Herman Pritchett, Henry A. Turner and Dean Mann American Democracy in World Perspective Fourth Edition, New York: Harper and Row (1976) 66.

37. Thomas R. Dye and L. Harmon Ziegler The Irony of Democracy: An Uncommon Introduction to American Politics Third Edition North Scituate, Mass.: Duxbury (1975) 58. See also James MacGregor Burns and J.W. Peltason with Thomas E. Cronin, Government by the People Ninth Edition Englewood Cliffs, N.J.: Prentice-Hall (1975) 53; Walter F. Murphy and Michael N. Danielson Robert K. Carr and Marver H. Bernstein's American Democracy Eighth Edition Hinsdale, Ill.: Dryden (1977) 94; Milton C. Cummings, Jr. and David Wise Democracy Under Pressure Third Edition New York: Harcourt Brace Jovanovich (1977) 48; Theodore J. Lowi American Government: Incomplete Conquest Hinsdale, Ill.: Dryden (1976) 105; Kenneth Prewitt and Sidney Verba An Introduction to American Government Second Edition New York: Harper & Row (1976) 369; Robert S. Ross American National Government Second Edition Chicago: Rand McNally (1976) 17; Raymond E. Wolfinger, Martin Shapiro and Fred I. Greenstein Dynamics of American Politics Englewood Cliffs, N.J.: Prentice-Hall (1976) 46.

38. David Easton A System Analysis of Political Life New York: John Wiley (1965) 26-33, 376-81; Gabriel A. Almond and G. Bingham Powell, Jr., Comparative Politics: A Developmental Approach Boston: Little, Brown (1966) 16-189; David C. Saffell The Politics of American

75

National Government Second Edition, Cambridge, Mass.: Winthrop (1975) 11-14; and Ira Sharkansky and Donald Van Meter Policy and Politics in American Governments New York: McGraw-Hill (1975) 6-11, 242.

39. Louis Loeb and Daniel M. Berman American Politics: Crisis and Challenge New York: Macmillan (1975) 363.

40. Prewitt and Verba op. cit. 301.

41. Dante Germino Modern Western Political Thought: Machiavelli to Marx Chicago: Rand McNally (1972) 150-73, 181; Jack C. Plano and Milton Greenberg The American Political Dictionary Third Edition Hinsdale, Ill.: Dryden (1972) 12.

42. A prize winning journalist expounds the theory that divided government is not responsible government. David S. Broder The Party's Over: The Failure of Politics in America New York: Harper and Row (1972).

43. Robert L. Keighton with Martin P. Sutton One Nation Lexington, Mass.: D.C. Heath (1972) 43.

44. Max J. Skidmore and Marshall Carter Wanke American Government: A Brief Introduction New York: St. Martin's (1974) 19. Similarly: "By constitutional design each branch of the system reflects different combinations of interests, and at any given time, those who want to block legislation have an advantage over those who seek to pass it." Robert H. Salisbury Governing America: Public Choice and Political Action New York: Appleton-Century-Crofts (1973) 201. See fns 9, 32 supra.

45. For instance, Aristotle proposed that balance of freedom and stability be sought by distributing governmental offices between oligarchic and democratic forces. Politics, IV, xic.

46. This is the essence of the "pluralist" concept of democracy contested by the "elitists." See infra The Legitimacy of Specialized Government—Specialized Representation.

47. See, for instance, Article VIII of the Massachusetts Bill of Rights, Articles III and V of the Virginia Bill of Rights, and Article VI of the Pennsylvania Declaration of Rights, Poore op. cit. 958, 1909, 1541.

48. ". . . congressmen like to play the role of humanizing the bureaucracy." Karl A. Lamb The People, Maybe Second Edition North Scituate, Mass.; Duxbury (1974) 160.

49. Georgia and Pennsylvania. The Georgia Council probably was more like a colonial period council (but with a weak governor) while the Pennsylvania one took the place of the governor as well.

50. May 31, 1787 and June 7, 1787.

51. The issue at this point was whether the lower house of the national legislature or the state legislatures should select the members of the upper house. (Remarks were made on June 7th.)

52. June 7, 1787. James Wilson apparently was the only delegate who favored popular election of the upper house at that time.

53. June 12, 1787. The debate issue was a seven or three year term for senators.

54. U.S. Cont., I, 8 (par. 18). The Convention avoided authorization of a cabinet on June 1, August 18, 20 and 22, and September 7, 1787.

55. Peter Woll Public Policy Cambridge, Mass.: Winthrop (1974) 29.

56. Edmund S. Morgan The Birth of the Republic 1763-1789 Chicago: University of Chicago Press (1956) 123-25.

57. U.S. Const. II, 2 (par. 1). Professor Corwin says that this clause "is the modest residuum of numerous efforts in the Convention of 1787 to load the President with a 'Council of State.' " Edward S. Corwin The President: Office and Powers Third Edition, New York: New York University Press (1948) 424, fn. 51. The clause apparently was one product of the committee of eleven, near the close of the Convention, Max Farrand The Framing of the Constitution of the United States. New Haven: Yale University (1913) 166.

58. U.S. Const. II, 2 (par. 2).

59. Humphrey's Executor v. United States 295 U.S. 602 (1935).

60. Erwin C. Hargrove The Power of the Modern Presidency Philadelphia: Temple University Press (1974) 237.

61. Rowland Egger The President of the United States Second Edition New York: McGraw-Hill (1972) 32; Dorothy B. James The Contemporary Presidency Second Edition Indianapolis: Bobbs-Merrill (1974) 204; Louis W. Koenig The Chief Executive Third Edition New York: Harcourt Brace Jovanovich (1975) 183; Peter Woll and Rochelle Jones "The Bureaucracy as a Check Upon the President" 3 Bureaucrat (April 1974) 8-20 at 17. See also Thomas E. Cronin The State of the Presidency Boston; Little, Brown (1975) 98 and Louis W. Koenig Congress and the President Chicago; Scott, Foresman (1965) 120.

62. Wayman v. Southard 10 Wheaton 1, 42 (1825).

63. United States v. Nixon 418 U.S. 683, 703, 704 (1974).

64. Ibid. 708.

65. Ibid. 706.

66. Ibid. 706, 707.

67. Ibid. 707.

68. Montesquieu L'Esprit des Lois XI, 6, pars. 55, 56.

69. Ebenstein, Pritchett, Turner and Mann op. cit. 66, 67.

70. Prewitt and Verba op. cit. 367.

71. Richard E. Neustadt "Presidential Government" International Encyclopedia of the Social Sciences New York: Macmillan (1968) 454.

72. See Unsystematic Recognition of Presidential-Administrative Separation, supra.

73. Bertram M. Gross The Legislative Struggle: A Study in Social Combat New York: McGraw-Hill (1953) 105.

74. Grant McConnell The Modern Presidency Second Edition New York: St. Martin's (1976) 65; similarly 1967 edition 56.

75. Philippa Strum Presidential Power and American Democracy Pacific Palisades, Calif.: Goodyear (1972) 43.

76. Cronin op. cit. 97.

77. One survey indicates that the career administrators during President Nixon's regime were more pro-welfare and perhaps more Democratic than the "political appointees" at the time. Joel D. Aberbach and Bert A. Rockman "Clashing Beliefs within the Executive Branch: The Nixon Administration Bureaucracy" 70 American Political Science Review (June 1976) 456-68.

78. Woll and Jones op. cit. (fn. 61) 20.

79. Rexford G. Tugwell "On Bringing Presidents to Heel" Rexford G. Tugwell and Thomas E. Cronin (Eds.) The Presidency Reappraised New

York: Praeger (1974) 266-93 at 267. Similarly, Second Edition (1977) 303.
    80. McConnell op. cit. 75.
    81. Peter Woll Public Policy Cambridge, Mass.: Winthrop (1974) 14,
15, 29; Robert C. Fried Performance in American Bureaucracy Boston:
Little, Brown (1976) 182-84; William L. Morrow Public Administration:
Politics and the Political System New York: Random House (1975) 170-71.

THE LEGITIMACY
OF SPECIALIZED GOVERNMENT

The third distinguishable pattern of distributed power in the American national government pertains to the specialized operating institutions. These units include the administrative bureaus and their subdivisions and also the specialized elements of the congressional and judicial branches. We will see that there is a good deal of relationship between comparable subunits of the different branches. Specialized government also involves semiofficial interactions with the particularized infrastructure of the socio-economic system of the nation, that is, governmental subunits tend to respond to the activated demands and supports of the organized subpublics.[1]

Specialized government may be a conglomerate more than a single entity but it is separately identifiable. Its constitutional status may be less explicit than that of the congressional, presidential and judicial structures, but it is persistently dominant in the multitudinous operations of the United States government.

This chapter will examine the legitimacy of specialized government. It will begin with a historical sketch of the primacy of departmentalization in the development of modern government. Then it will outline the forces of specialization in the organization of Congress, and in the functions of representation and legislation. Next it will consider specialization in the operation and the control of administrative units. The final section will examine relationships between the governmental subunits and the specialized publics of the politico-economic society.

The Primacy of Departmentalized Administration

The evolution of centralized national governments from decentralized feudal systems entailed the development of administrative as well as legislative structures. In fact, the administrative units achieved the strength of continuity in advance of the representative legislative institutions. For instance, the Norman kings developed efficient financial administration even before the conquest of England; then they held sway over the English barons through centralized operations.[2] Departmentalization increased through the centuries. Henry I (1100-1135) was a "cold, shrewd" administrator; [3] while the Angevins, beginning with Henry II (1154-1189), established a national or common system of courts which had a mixture of judicial and administrative specializations.[4] On the other hand, the development of the English parliaments came in the next century, and then the sessions were more irregular than periodic.[5] Moreover, the parliaments were channels of communication for the king more than for the taxpayers, that is, the flow was more down than up. Even the "model Parliament" of 1295 was primarily to support the need of Edward I (1272-1307) for more revenue.

The efforts of the early parliaments seem to have been more retrospective correction than prospective direction. "Legislation was no part of Parliament's functions," C. R. Lovell points out in his study of English constitutional and legal history. He recognizes that one might "argue that parliamentary judicial work on petitions was legislative in a sense," but he asserts that "such a view is not really justifiable" because "this work merely meant sending cases to particular courts or issuing bills in eyre."[6] In fact, Parliament was a "court" before it was a "legislature."[7] "Not one of the great statutes of Edward I was the result of parliamentary actions," Professor Lovell observes. He explains that the king might occasionally consult with interested groups but that "he was under no obligation to do so." Yet administration and adjudication already were specialized. Besides a chancellor and a treasury, there were separate courts, notably Common Pleas, Exchequer, and the King's Bench.[8]

There is relevance, some political scientists find, in Winston Churchill's account of Henry I's use of "royal servants who were members of the minor baronage" to "act as a brake upon the turbulence of the greater feudatories." Churchill points out that that event marked "the first beginnings . . . of a civil administrative machinery, which within its limits was more efficient and persistent than anything yet known." Churchill adds that these officials "developed a vested interest of their own," and created what was in fact an official class.[9] Some persons may have similar views of today's specialized administrators.

Historical analysis of administrative government also shows a uniform pattern in the inevitable development of specialization. Virtually every government of any size or degree of advancement has embodied similar areas of subject specialization. One scholarly study of "the profession of government" concludes that there have been five fields of administration, that is, foreign affairs, military, justice, finance and internal affairs, in almost every government of historical note.[10] Today, the United States has several departments for internal affairs; but that is true of most countries, including Germany and Great Britain and, to an even larger degree, the U.S.S.R. and China. There is probably more similarity among governments in their types of administrative structures than in the kinds of higher political institutions.[11]

In the United States, there is a definite historical priority of specialized administration to general policy institutions. Looking at the steps to our national political identity, we had Committees of Correspondence before we had Continental Congresses, or the Articles of Confederation. Moreover, we had an administrative bureau before the Declaration of Independence; Benjamin Franklin became Postmaster

General in July 1775. The necessity of a post office and other means of political communication to the attainment of our national statehood is early proof of the essentially interactive character of a successful political system.[12]

There was definite correlation between the establishment of administrative departments and our development of national strength. We had executive departments before we had an executive president. In 1781, the Congress of the Confederation established departments of foreign affairs, war and finance, each of which generally was headed by a single officer. Those in charge of foreign affairs included Robert Livingston, who later negotiated the Louisiana purchase, and John Jay, who afterwards served as ambassador to England and became the first chief justice. Robert Morris, in charge of finance, was a man of great skill and strong action. His irritation of Congress caused his replacement by a three man commission for the final years of the Confederation. The continuity of the departments throughout the period of constitutional change is evidenced by the career of Henry Knox. Formerly a general in the independence war, he was head of the Department of War from 1785 to 1794, that is, from four years before the adoption of the new Constitution until four years afterwards.[13]

The workers in these departments "became the first professional civil servants in the United States." Many of them "continued to work in the same capacities under the new government after the Confederation ended."[14] For instance, Joseph Nourse of Virginia was register of the treasury from 1781 to 1829 while Henry Remsen held a succession of offices under the Confederation government and then served as chief clerk of the Department of State until he resigned in 1792.[15] Thus, there was a continuity of administrative personnel even with a change of constitutions similar to the present day practice of career officials remaining while presidents come and go. This is further evidence of the inevitability of specialized administration and the continuity of less publicized officials.

The 1789 Congress, acting under the "necessary and proper" clause for "carrying into Execution" all powers vested in the government "or in any department or officer thereof," continued the three departments which had existed from 1781. Foreign Affairs, with added domestic duties, was named the Department of State, and the new War department included naval and Indian affairs. Congress called the financial office the Department of the Treasury. Interestingly, it designated the first two "executive departments" but not the third. It also made the Secretary of the Treasury and several other top officials of that institution directly answerable to the houses of Congress. This may reflect the close relationship which state legislatures at the time felt toward state treasurers. In fact, the national Convention of 1787 until almost its last day gave Congress authority to select a national treasurer. The new government in 1789 established the office of Attorney General. That official was immediately a member of the cabinet but the office was not departmentalized until decades later.

81

The growth of the departmental structure was slow at first but then came in spurts. The Navy became a separate department in 1798; the Department of Interior, with functions from State and War, was established in 1849; and, in two decades, 1870-89, Justice, the Post Office and Agriculture were departmentalized. A Department of Commerce and Labor came into being in 1903 and became two departments in 1913. The military departments were united into a Department of Defense in 1947. The Department of Health, Education and Welfare was fabricated in 1953, Housing and Urban Development in 1965 and Transportation in 1966. The Post Office became a government corporation in 1970[16] and a Department of Energy was established in 1977.

Congress began to establish special courts in the 1850s and independent regulatory commissions in the 1880s.

There are now at least fifty operating agencies outside any department. About ten of these are in the Executive Office of the President. The others are classed officially as Independent Agencies.

The congressional actions which have contributed most to the evolution of presidential-administrative separation may be those establishing and extending the Civil Service and other merit systems. This development began in 1883 and now most of the civilian employees of the national government are under some type of such procedure.[17]

The Departmentalization of Congress

The underlying force of subject specialization in modern government is evident not only in the administrative departments but also in the extent to which particularized committees dominate decision making in the legislative chambers. In fact, the committee system in Congress developed as an early response to the departmentalization of the executive leadership. The center of interest was the formulation of congressional policies on finances. When the new constitutional government began in 1789 Alexander Hamilton, as Secretary of the Treasury, worked closely with the leaders of Congress, and they relied upon his famous reports on taxes, banking and tariffs. After he left the cabinet, the House of Representatives formed a committee of Ways and Means to prepare reports and projects as Hamilton had done. When Thomas Jefferson became president, he named Albert Gallatin to the Treasury post. Gallatin had been a leader of the lower house, and he was as accomplished in many ways as Hamilton. He held the confidence of the congressional leaders and presented reports and programs on finances. As a consequence the Ways and Means committee languished. But when Gallatin ceased to have command of the situation and then left the cabinet, the House of Representatives again turned to the committee on Ways and Means for its information and policies on finances and taxes.[18]

"The growth of congressional committees has largely paralleled the growth of the bureaucracy. In much the same way that demand for governmental services, on the one hand, or regulation, on the other hand, has spawned executive agencies, so also has it resulted in the creation of congressional committees."[19] There is noticeable similarity of functional specialization between the committees of the two houses and the administrative structures.

The comparability is greater for the older and more general departments than for the newer and more specialized units. There are committees in each house corresponding to the departments of State Defense, and Justice. Each house also has two committees (for banking and for taxation) relating to the activities of Treasury. There were committees in each house paralleling the departments of Interior, Agriculture, Commerce and Labor, but a good deal of the symmetry has vanished. Neither house established corresponding committees when the department of Health, Education and Welfare, then Housing and Urban Development, and finally Transportation were formed. Rather, they continued to assign these areas to other committees, such as Public Works, Commerce, Labor or Banking. Another disturbing factor came with the start of the 95th Congress in 1977. The Senate, to reduce the number of its committees, changed the Interior committee to Energy and Natural Resources and the Labor committee to Human Resources, as well as making other re-arrangements.[20] The House made no similar changes in 1977.

The development which is probably most important from the viewpoint of specialized government is the increase during recent decades in the number and power of subcommittees. Each house now has more than a hundred and they allow more members the opportunity to enjoy the prestige and power of a committee chairmanship.

Richard E. Neustadt explains the close relationship of administrative fragmentation to congressional committee specialization. "Congress, constitutionally, has at least as much to do with executive administration as does an incumbent of the White House." He points out that "four tangible, indispensable administrative powers rest with Congress: organization, authorization, financing and investigation." By their use Congress provides the departments and agencies with operational authority, programmic jurisdiction, funds and "oversight."[21] Congressional action tends to be particular because of its own composition, he explains. "Had Congress been a unit tightly organized and centrally directed, its employment of these powers might have brought us something comparable at the other end of Pennsylvania Avenue: a unified executive establishment," Neustadt points out. "But actually, and naturally, what was produced 'downtown' reflects congressional *disunity*." Congressional prerogatives are exercised "piecemeal, on the executive establishment downtown. Its character is shaped accordingly."

"Both organizationally and in terms of personnel the new bureaucracy is a projection of congressional committee jurisdictions--or, more precisely, since 1946, of standing subcommittee jurisdictions," Neustadt adds.

"Why, for example, is the Small Business Administration independent of the Department of Commerce? The answer lies in the committee structure of the House." He recognizes that administrative developments sometimes influence committee jurisdiction—unification of the armed services was matched by unification of the corresponding committees. "Still, the pattern remains one in which particular committees deal with given agencies, and thereby keep the agencies distinct from one another," Neustadt concludes.[22]

Political science explanations of American national government recognize decentralization of power in Congress in much the same degree that they acknowledge subsystem autonomy in the administrative system. They associate congressional fragmentation with the power of the chairmen and the ranking minority members of the leading committees and subcommittees. Recently, the seniority rule has lost some of its force. The party caucus may make exceptions. But there are other factors which enhance decentralization of power. The number of subcommittees has increased. Unbalanced party systems in home districts and states continue to aid long tenure and to strengthen singular viewpoints.[23] The operating power of committee leaders derives from several factors. These include their expertise, the control over the flow of legislation, the mutual deference system in the houses, clientele relationships with executive agencies and interest groups, and public hearings.[24] There is an underlying appreciation of specialization and expertise,[25] and sometimes respect extends beyond the particular area of specialization.[26]

Mutual deference is the key to whatever unity either house possesses. Congress, a former Representative asserts, is "a collection of committees that come together in a Chamber periodically to approve one another's actions." Outside observers see even less coherence. One political science explanation declares that because Congress operates largely through committees, "it is almost impossible to speak of Congress as a whole," except occasionally when there is "a high degree of unanimity at governmental and private levels." The explanation concludes that "there is no collective congressional intent; there is only the intent of many individuals and groups within Congress."[27] The same may be said of the executive branch. Mutual deference may be the key to whatever unity it possesses.

Specialized Representation

The Constitutional Convention of 1787 evidently assumed that many problems of government relate directly to the aggressive factions of the politico-economic society. The Convention delegates were much concerned with the manner in which the houses of Congress, and in a lesser degree the presidency, would reflect the competitive interests of the nation. The last chapter reviewed the ways in which the Convention applied the idea of mixed representation, that is, it gave the "popular" landed interests--the family farmers meeting the property voting requirements--control over the election of the House of Representatives and the commercial and financial interests indirect dominion through the state legislatures over the choice of the Senators.[28]

At the Convention, James Madison pointed out that nationalizing the government would bring a larger number of "factions" into active competition against a potentially tyrannical majority. Madison noted that every society has "different Sects, Factions, and interests," such as the rich, poor, debtors, creditors, landed, manufacturing and commercial. "The only remedy," he said, "is to enlarge the sphere" (to national size) and have "so great a number of interests and parties" that a majority will not be able to pursue a "common interest." (June 6, 1787). A similar dialogue occurred later (June 25, 26, 1787).[29] The tenth letter of The Federalist also deals with the interplay of factions and their potential effect upon the majority in the legislature as well as upon each other.

Political scientists have spent much time debating whether the process of competitive factions or groups is democratic. The answers seem more circumstantial than essential, that is, that its merit depends considerably upon the extent of participation. But that is also true of the electoral process. Voting became more democratic as the suffrage widened and more persons exercised that privilege.

Our interest here is not primarily whether the group process is actually a democratic system but rather whether it has a place in the constitutional pattern of distribution. In other words, does it add another dimension to the principle and practice of checks and balances? Madison apparently had in mind the impact of the factions upon the legislature but there is also the matter of their impact upon the operating units of the government, either directly or through the members of the Congress. Madison was interested in their restraining force but they also have potential innovating and motivating power. Their more positive actions can be directed at the executive units as well as the legislators. Here we are concerned with the constitutional as well as the political and practical legitimacy. Specialized representation is a means of organizing demands and supports and bringing them into the system of checks and balances.

Probably no aspect of the American social-governmental system is more analyzed and debated by political scientists of today than the quality of special interest organizations. Yet scholarly acknowledgement of their political influence is not at all new. Social analysts were aware of specialized input pressures long before James Madison argued the restraining force of a multiplicity of factions. An essay published in 1741 by David Hume, the Scottish philosopher-historian, classified factions involved in the political process. He distinguished personal from real factions and associated the former with small republics. There are, he said, three kinds of real factions--those based upon interest, those based upon principle and those grounded upon affection. He observed that we accept differences in interest, such as economic preferences, more easily then differences in principle, such as religious beliefs or faiths.[30]   The entire analysis seems to emphasize sociological factors.

Jean Jacques Rousseau dealt with factions in his 1762 Social Contract. He explained that "when cabals and partial associations are formed at the expense of the great association, the will of each association, though *general* with regard to its members, is *private* with regard to the state." He asserted that to obtain expression of the general will of the state, "no partial society should be formed in the State." "When there are partial societies, it is politic to multiply their number, that they may be all kept on an equality." Thus, he preceded Madison in suggesting that the general will, or the common good, be aided and that irrationality be reduced, by pitting special interests against each other. Yet Rousseau claimed no originality; he noted that the method had been pursued by Solon, Numa and Servius.[31]

The. nineteenth century brought public and academic prestige to special interest activities. The American tendency to form associations, identified by de Tocqueville, in his Democracy in America (1830), made minority groups seem appropriate in an open and individualistic society. Later, the growth of particular industries led to government regulation. Then the emergence of labor unions, in opposition to business forces, brought a proliferation of unofficial confrontations that in extreme situations entered the governmental conflict-resolution process. Developments in sociology and group psychology made specialized political activity seem more respectable.[32]

The political science discipline in the United States gave increasing attention to the group process from about 1930 and by the 1950s multiplicity of input channels joined separation of output actions as a test of legitimacy.[33]

Now, virtually all American government texts give interest groups a key role. But they differ in the depth of analysis, appraisal of impact and classificatory terminology. Compositely, the texts differentiate among six general types: "social groups," mainly religious and fraternal, which are value protective; "special interest groups," mainly income protective, such as labor, business, or professional associations which compete among themselves; "political interest or pressure groups," mainly special interest groups which endeavor to influence governmental decisions more or less directly; "public interest groups," which tend to have broader concern, such as consumer interests; "governmental pressure groups," which are bureaus, committees, or other entities with a concentrated self-protective mode of activity; and "potential interest groups," which may arise among under-privileged persons when conditions of awareness and leadership are more developed.

Political scientists disagree, sometimes sharply, on whether the effect of the interest group system upon government is elitist and non-democratic or pluralist and democratic.[34]   The conflict has divergent causes--contrasting attitudes toward equality and liberty as well as varying assumptions about the extent of participation. The consensus seems to be that roughly a third of the adult males belong to no organized association and that another third belong to groups which use little or no pressure upon government.[35] Pressure groups differ in their inclination and their capacity to influence public decisions, but political scientists tend to agree that internal organization is often elitist, and that the system aids the "haves" more than the "have-nots." During the past decade there has been an increase in group representation of minorities and the under-privileged. There are also more associations which exert pressure for "public interests," such as environmental and consumer protection.[36] The system, even though less elitist, still shows the force of particularized organization. Congressional and administrative subunits tend to respond more to persons with group representation than to those without such support.

Specialized Legislation

The most consequential role of the members of Congress may not be to confront the presidency or the courts in a public drama of strong assertions of unified policy, nor may it be to act as internal parts of two coherent political parties or even to be members of fifteen or twenty standing committees; rather it may be to guide and restrain the specialized operations of the administrative branch in relation to the demands and supports of the multiplicity of diverse groups--potential as well as actual--which make up the national society. This may mean that the legislative process is not so much the enactment of general, prospective statutes as the readjustment of particular sets of legal rules on a more or less continuous basis as retrospective surveillance of agencies and bureaus may warrant. In other words, the essential and relevant function of Senators and Representatives may be to act in small groups--preferably bipartisan or otherwise politically balanced--in conjunction with the corresponding subunits of the group structured society and the agency structured administration.

The character of these specialized reviews of applied law may mean that the congressional committees or subcommittees are similar to specialized appellate tribunals. They lack the technical methods of judicial courts, of course, but they are retrospective and particular in passing corrective judgment upon the policy and decision making of specialized administrators.

This view of the legislative process is not stated neatly or definitely in any official document but it seems to be the import of the efforts of political scientists to describe the American national government in its entirety. The centers of power are primarily the subcommittees of the houses of Congress as they are related to the administrative bureaus and the group lobbyists.

A few decades ago, Woodrow Wilson called the standing committees, the "little legislatures of Congress" and recently a political scientist, George Goodwin Jr., called the subcommittees, "the miniature legislatures of Congress."[37] Richard Neustadt makes a point of this transition in his 1973 analysis of legislative-administrative relationships.[38]

The increase in the number and importance of subcommittees has broadened the pragmatic power structure of Congress because it allows more Senators and Representatives to have a piece of the action, positive or negative, as it may be. That has brought the benefits of the seniority rule to more members, particularly those in the middle age brackets. Each house has more than a hundred subcommittees and while some members may hold two chairmanships, the total number allows a wide distribution. In the Senate, during recent years, every member of the majority party (Democratic) with as much as two years service, has been a chairman of some standing subcommittee.

Most political science explanations of the American national government recognize the special potentials of subcommittee chairman.[39] These include the opportunities to build public prestige and an activist image through hearings and investigations with respect to proposed legislation, operating performance, and general matters of public anxiety.

Subcommittees make the primary and most detailed analysis of proposed legislation and their recommendations often are the basis of action (or nonaction) by the respective chamber. Parent committees tend to accept subcommittee reports and the full chamber usually respects the recommendation of the standing committees.[40] There are exceptions, of course, and naturally they are likely to receive the most media coverage, but deference among subcommittees may be the principal key to congressional behavior.[41] The specialized diversity of the hundred or more subcommittees in each house may be an index to the fragmentation at the politico-governmental frontier.

The specificity and diversity of contemporary legislation is shown by the "titles" in the United States Code and the Code of Federal Regulations. The one code is a systematic compilation of statutory enactments and the other is an annual publication of administrative regulations. Each code has approximately fifty "titles." Many are similar; in total, there are about sixty different subjects. A few concern general matters, such as Congress, the presidency, and government accounting, personnel and organization, but most titles relate to a substantive specialization. Some titles pertain to the independent agencies, and there are more than one for most departments. For instance, five titles (Indians, parks and forests, minerals and mining, public lands, and wildlife and fisheries) concern the Department of Interior; four titles (education, food and drugs, public health and public welfare) relate to H E W; while five titles (banks and banking, custom duties, internal revenue, intoxicating liquors, and money and finance) concern the Treasury. These titles are one identification of the "subsystems" which compose the less visible portion of the governmental iceberg.[42]

Specialization among members of Congress has not eliminated heavy reliance upon bureaucratic expertise in the processes of legislation. Even basic political science texts recognize that administrative specialists are partners with legislative committees. "In almost any area of national policy, legislators lack the bureaucrat's expertise," one text explains. It asserts that, contrary to the "public" belief, "fully three-quarters of all legislation originates with the bureaucracy."[43] Another political science volume gives this explanation: "The complex problems of modern society encourage legislatures to enact laws in more and more general terms, indicating broad lines of policy and leaving details to other governmental agencies."[44] There are also specific examples. For instance, "in the case of automobile safety standards, all that Congress did was to recognize that standards were necessary, but it relinquished the responsibility of devising them."[45] Then in the field of education the relevant subcommittees of Congress are likely to work with the Office of Education.[46] Another reason for congressional dependence upon administrative rule making is the desire to avoid political conflicts—"very often congressmen omit certain details from legislation in order to avoid taking a positive stand on a controversial issue."[47]

These observations show that the specialized administrators are coordinate legislators. General political science explanations still present the constitutional ideology of three separate powers, but their explanations of regular operations show that a four branch model of government is often more truly informative than the traditional three branch model.

Specialized Administration

The members of the president's cabinet are keystone figures in the constrast between the ideology of executive branch unity and the actual administrative disunity among and within the departments.

The cabinet, without express constitutional or even statutory authorization, is next to the presidency in the popular association of the government with the images of the Founders. The first cabinet, with Thomas Jefferson and Alexander Hamilton in opposition, has a higher place in our political tradition than the first Congress, even though the latter was in effect an "overtime" constitutional convention. The confrontation of Jefferson and Hamilton personifies the continuing antithesis in the American economic society as well as our unsinkable two party system.

The first cabinet was the scene of the initial debate on the scope of the Constitution. The narrow and broad theories of interpretation confronted each other on the authority of the national government to establish the Bank of the United States. No cabinet since then has had such dimensions and it remains an ideological model even if never actually duplicated. Washington's second term cabinet was picked much more for agreement with presidential perspectives. So have all its successors.

Cabinets tend to reflect the diverse elements of the political spectrum. Usually, the different members can be identified with the principal regions, the major economic sectors, and the foremost sociological groups of the country. At times, one belongs formally to the opposite party. Now, a Catholic, a Jew, a Black, and a Lady are vital. Thus, the members form a coalition of "access images." They stand for channels of communication from major interests of the nation to the person in the Oval Office. However, the majority of cabinet members learn sooner or later that they have less meaningful access to the president than the White House assistants and advisers.

The cabinet collectively may not participate in the formation of presidential policies to any substantial degree. Meetings of the full cabinet are apt to be formal[48] and to provide the president means of airing his own selected thoughts. Inner cabinet members may contribute to policy formulation but that is mostly on an individual basis. Collectively, the cabinet has "only a symbolic value" which "readily disappears when the need for action supersedes the need for a show window."[49] Presidents Nixon, Ford and Carter each began with the idea of making the cabinet a stronger, more active and more public policy maker[50] but little basic change developed.

Presidents are forced more and more to draw upon the Executive Office-White House-inner circle. "Domestic crises and critical international developments . . . soon begin to monopolize the presidential schedule."[51] Under pressure for timely actions, a president looks to his closest advisers and assistants and the White House staff begins to "outstrip most of the cabinet in power and influence."[52] Professor Neustadt puts the matter in sharp focus. "Trying to stop fires is what Presidents do first. It takes most of their time," he asserts.[53] Professor Vinyard explains that a president "must deal with those matters he considers most important or urgent or troublesome, leaving much of the bureaucracy free to operate at the discretion of its administrators."[54]

Cabinet members, as heads of their respective departments, tend to develop considerable independence of the White House. Professor Gawthrop states that no matter "how much conscious deliberation an incoming President gives to the selection of his departmental secretaries, each of them will inevitably become a 'chief executive' in his own right."[55] Harold Seidman, one-time management specialist in the Bureau of the Budget, points out that the "outer cabinet" members become particularly concerned with internal administrative relationships.[56] The head of a department may draw away from the presidency because of increasing deference to Congress on which he must depend for final budget approval and for statutory enactments.[57]

A department head also may lack effective control over lower officials.[58] Professor Koenig calls attention to the centrifugal forces. "Just as the President faces great difficulty in controlling policymaking by his departments, the department secretary is faced with an array of bureaus not uncommonly in a state of incipient or actual mutiny."[59]   He faces a "major dilemma" in choosing between the presidency and his bureaucratic support.[60]   One new department head likened himself to a sea captain who had never seen his ship before and did not know its mechanism, its officers or its crew. "Cabinet secretaries come and go; the civil service remains." In fact, the "expert technician" who has been in charge of a bureau for many years "may resent the effort of a political appointee to take control of his bureau."[61]   Professor Gawthrop says that "the federal executive bureaucracy is a composite set of semiautonomous subunits," and that "as the delegation of authority increases in the executive branch, the power to control organizational behavior becomes increasingly fragmented, dispersed and unequal." [62]

Specialized Control of Administrative Functions

The factors which cause separation of the continuing administrative realm from the presidential executive forces may be strongest at the level of the specialized subunits.   It is there that continuing professional expertise is most needed for dealing with the millions of persons who have obligatory or beneficial relationships with the government. It is also there that the political or professional pressures of special interest groups are most immense and often most intense. Moreover, it is in relation to the activities of the operating units that Senators and Representatives receive the most specific complaints and appeals from their constituents.

The main focus of most congressional and judicial surveillance is the protection of individual and group interests. They receive more oversight attention than the "public welfare" or even the common good of the active electorate of the majority party. The specialized control of administrative functions shows more respect for the way in which the rights and duties of particular persons are determined than for improving public projects or supervising public property and institutions.[63]

The foremost effort to assure fair protection for the rights of individuals, at least when represented by an attorney or other agent familiar with judicial type procedure, was the adoption of the Administrative Procedure Act in 1947.[64]   The aim was to make sure that all operating agencies with regulatory type of functions conformed to the basic procedural standards of the Anglo-American judicial system.   Many administrative units had adopted equitable procedures before its enactment but that statute sought to ensure that all agencies met minimum standards. The Act defines three principal terms, that is, "agency," "rule," and "order." It gives each a broad meaning. "Agency" stands for any authority of the government other than Congress, the federal courts, or the governments of the District of Columbia, or any territory or possession.   A leading administrative law professor, Kenneth Culp Davis, explains that it means "a governmental authority, other than a court and other than a legislative body, which affects the rights of private parties through either adjudication or rule making." [65]

The Act defines a "rule" to be an "agency statement of general or particular applicability and future effect designed to implement, or prescribe law or policy or describing the organization, procedure, or practice requirements of any agency." Thus a rule has the basic qualities of a law, that is, it is general and prospective. The Act requires that agency rules be published and that advance notice be given of contemplated changes. Current publication is in The Federal Register while the accumulated rules are published in each year's edition of The Code of Federal Regulations. The diversity and immensity of that code were described earlier in this chapter. It is probably the principal body of rules which allows us to have a "government by laws" in contrast to a "government by men." But it also increases considerably the need for special representation before administrative units, courts, and subcommittees of Congress.

Many enactments of Congress basically may be more adjudicative (or particular and retrospective) than legislative (or general and prospective), that is, they may correct a previous enactment by adjusting that law to meet newly recognized conditions. For example, the laws with respect to internal revenue, society security, farm support, or civil rights, may be under almost constant reconsideration with some kind of change at frequent intervals. Often agencies may be able to meet congressional complaints, expressed at subcommittee hearings or through informal channels, by revising their own regulations, but other times enactments by Congress may be necessary.

The extreme example of legislation-in-form-but-not-in-substance is probably the "private bill." Congress enacts a few hundred of these in each session. Yet, they do not meet the essential test of a law; they are not general and prospective but particular and retrospective. One example is the cancellation of a monetary claim because its collection would be unconscionable, such as a bill to an Army sergeant for equipment not accounted for many years previously. Another example is an adjustment to immigration or nationalization rules to allow a scientist to remain in the United States for special research purposes. The "private bill" does not violate the ban on bills of attainder or ex post facto laws because it is beneficial and not detrimental to an individual. But it means that Congress is deciding, or more accurately, reversing an administrative application of a law, not by passing general legislation, but by acting like an appellate court reviewing particular actions by the government. Congress, like a court, may be guided by a higher law of conscience or justice. Political science explanations of congressional processes and of the national government generally rarely mention the "private bill" procedure. The actions may seem minor and non-controversial but they are pointed instances of administrative review and reversal by Congress.

The houses of Congress, or more directly, their committees and subcommittees, also engage in much quasi-adjudicative investigation. They seldom use the high level procedure of impeachment of civil officers by the House of Representatives and trial by the Senate; in fact, only judges have been removed after such a trial. But they do hold numerous inquiries which judge private and public behavior retrospectively. Every year Congress holds more than two hundred investigations, ranging from a few spectacular televised hearings to routine unpublicized reviews of many areas of government.

Congressional investigations are not adjudicative in a strict sense because they do not decide any person's criminal or civil liability; but they may be indirectly detrimental to witnesses and others. They are more adjudicative than legislative in a general sense because they usually are retrospective and particular in their design. Moreover, Congress can require sworn testimony under criminal penalty for refusing to answer pertinent questions;[66] and the privilege against self-incrimination apparently is the only valid defense for those without "executive privilege." The Supreme Court in 1959 gave the congressional power to investigate as much constitutionality and legitimacy as it did the powers of legislation and appropriation.[67]

Those political science explanations of American government which have their publication roots in the 1950s seem to have the fullest analysis of the investigative power. The newer works either pass it by or merely refer to the most spectacular investigations, such as the Kefauver and McCarthy hearings of the 1950s and the Vietnam and Watergate ones.[68] The general import of the political science description of the investigative process is that it is an established part of the congressional surveillance of operating units.[69] A few analyses take the position that oversight of administration may be surpassing legislation as the prime function of the modern Congress.[70]

The foremost manifestation of specialized control of administrative functions is the unofficial multiplicity of "triple alliances," each composed of a few members of Congress, interest group spokesmen and an administrator. There are probably hundreds of such arrangements, existing informally and perhaps spasmodically, in the less visible and more technical operations of the government. They are seldom in the headlines because their actions are not very newsworthy. In fact, their power to control may depend upon keeping out of the top headlines because presidents tend to concentrate upon the most publicized issues. Political science specialists on the national executive generally call attention to their pervasive power.[71]

Many of the general political science explanations of the American national government recognize in some manner the specialized oversight or surveillance of administrative units by subcommittees or informal groups of members of Congress. Several volumes expressly refer to the threefold interaction of legislators, administrators and lobbyists.[72] Others add such competing forces as the presidency, public opinion, or the courts.[73] Still others point out that the rivalry between the White House and Capitol Hill allows the administrators much leeway in choosing their sources of support.[74]

Relationships with the Specialized Publics

The constitutional function of presidential-administrative separation involves not only its reinforcement of the principle of checks and balances, but also its contribution to the pluralistic resolution of specialized conflicts in Congress and in the national society. In such relationships, policy making is much like particularized adjudication. It also entails the First Amendment rights of private persons to associate together and to petition the government. This correspondence of governmental and socio-economic forces is described by William L. Morrow in his volume on public administration: [75]

> The conglomeratelike structural and operational character of public agencies is due to the heterogeneity of inputs directed toward such agencies. This characteristic represents most basically the unplanned, unsystematic way the American political system has dealt with policy problems. Agency form and jurisdiction represent formal expressions of organizational correctives designed to solve or alleviate social problems.

Thus, the specialized pattern of the administrative structure reflects that of the socio-economic organization. The latter may not be fully democratic but constitutional legitimacy is, of course, distinct from democratic quality. The constitutionality of a function tends to concern the availability of means more than the purposes of use. For instance, freedom of expression, right of petition, the privilege of voting, and freedom of association are constitutional vehicles, but whether they are democratic depends upon the manner and the extent of their use. The same is so of specialized means of conflict-resolution.

This consideration of the relationship between specialized government and particularized accommodation may be distinguished from the pluralist-elitist argument among political scientists. The point there is whether the group interest process makes the American government democratic or not. Here the issue is whether it is one of the elements in the pattern of authority distribution. We have seen that James Madison did consider the multiple faction phenomenon to be a part of the check-and-balance system. He indicated that the counteraction of mixed groups would restrain a possible tyranny of the majority in the House of Representatives. Nowadays, it might be a check upon a potentially imperial president.

Constitutional legitimacy does not require an activist or even a positive consequence. Its historical association often has been inaction or negation. Madison's objective was restrictive; he feared radicalism in the House; and at the same time he felt that the Senate and a presidential veto would not provide sufficient check. The general aim of constitutionalism has been, by a number of methods, to limit and to restrict. Constitutions arose to lessen arbitrary action; they endeavored to do this by distributing authority among different forces, and by giving counteracting institutions mutual negatives upon each other. In 1787, nearly two centuries ago, government was assumed to be primarily detrimental and coercive. Then there was merit in or need for limitation and constraint. Now, the commonest assumption is that government is or should be constructive and beneficial. Yet that change is more disturbing to the doctrines of separate and balanced powers than to competitive specialization. This last has a larger place in positive and corrective government. It is closer to the living conditions of today than the better known doctrines of three power government, pure or mixed. Likewise, it can contribute more to the task of keeping government within the public ideals of the political system than the more renowned theories of constitutional arrangement.

Even without consideration of these positive potentials, the separate administrative branch, composed as it is of heterogeneous units and supported by special interest associations, fits appropriately within the constitutional pattern of distribution. It does not determine criminal liability in any final manner and hence does not contravene the strict theory of separate legislative, executive and judicial functions. It does not encroach upon the excluded area of the "strictly and exclusively legislative." If there are similar sacred areas of executive and judicial powers, there is still a considerable volume of executive and judicial functions which the various specialized bureaus themselves may regularly undertake. The administrative branch performs legislative and judicial functions; and it has relations with Congress and the courts as well as those with the presidency. As a three function institution it serves three official masters and has the pragmatic autonomy of that position. A number of leading analysts consider the administrative branch to be in some measure free of control by any of the three other branches.[76] In that respect, it is, like the others, a coordinate branch with relationships of interdependence.

The problem of "democratic" legitimacy seems to concern both the appointed officialdom and the interest group system. A few political scientists have suggested that the career civil service is more representative than the elected officials because of a broader pattern of social origins and education.[77] But that may or may not tell us about their decision making attitudes. Sometimes persons with lower class origins develop a middle or upper class perspective.

The effect of special interest pressures may be a stronger force and it is not likely to be "democratic." Group representation seems to have about the same range as voter participation. Exercising the rights to join an association or to petition the government may be more difficult than casting a ballot but the percentage of formal group membership seems roughly equal to that of voting in the major elections.[78] A more substantial analogy may be to primary elections where a fraction of the potential voters often decides the outcome. The electoral system in its use is not fully "democratic" but no one questions the constitutionality of even primary elections.

Both electoral and group participation are much broader today than they were in Madison's time. Particularly in the past decade, there has been an increase in group organization among the less privileged and among those seeking to protect consumer and environmental rights. [79] Correspondingly, there have been more congressional subcommittees and administrative agencies in those areas. The record may not satisfy those who demand categorical change but it is at the level of the specialized institutions that continuing improvement is most likely. Thus, the least explicit pattern of governmental arrangement may provide the most enduring advancement.

Wider public participation in the interest group pressures upon specialized administrators could be beneficial to the higher levels of executive officials. It could permit the assistant secretaries of the departments, the members of the cabinet, and the Executive Office leaders, as well as the White House inner circle, to devote more time and effort to general problems and programs. In this way, it could increase the effectiveness of a president and his immediate advisers, in reconciling public demands and in establishing priorities among expectations and standards. It might even allow the presidents to concentrate upon the conflict of ideals rather than upon the competing interests among the specialized publics.

The public recognition of the presidential-administrative separation within the formal executive branch may be the first step in developments which could increase the effectiveness of presidents in the higher and more important functions. Democratic duties may include, not only voting, but also active participation in the specialized pressure system. Continuous public involvement needs to be directed at the higher levels of appointed officials as well as at the elected representatives. If we demand less from presidents in the management of particular operations we could expect more White House attention to broader policies and more general objectives. External relationships with the public and with other nations are higher in the scale of presidential priorities than the supervision of particular bureaus or agencies. Thus, the idea as well as the fact of a coordinate administrative branch, answerable directly to the other branches and the specialized publics, may help to elevate the role of the presidency. [80]

NOTES

1. Even some general political science explanations of the national government expressly recognize the relationship of the Constitution to social and governmental specialization. " . . . separation of powers is an organic part of a subtle constitutional system, needing other parts of the system for its own operation and itself in turn necessary to their functioning . . . separation of powers depends upon the multiplicity of interests which lessens the likelihood of majority factions. . . . At the same time, the very existence of the independent branches tends to foster

the necessary multiplicity." Martin Diamond, Winston Mills Fisk and Herbert Garfinkel, The Democratic Republic: An Introduction to American National Government Second Edition, Chicago: Rand, McNally (1971) 111. "The Constitution has had a lot to do with the evolution of the bureaucracy even in the absence of specific provision for it . . . . the bureaucracy . . . . reflects the diversity of the dominant elites. The bureaucracy's internal conflicts are the elite's conflicts." David J. Olson and Philip Meyer To Keep the Republic: Governing the United States in its Third Century New York: McGraw-Hill (1975) 392. The final statement makes reference to Peter Woll American Bureaucracy New York: W. W. Norton (1963).

2. Bryce Lyon A Constitutional and Legal History of Medieval England New York: Harper and Bros. (1960) 135, 138. "The efficiently organized central administration of the Normans is proof of their genius as organizers . . . Ibid. 166.

3. Colin R. Lovell English Constitutional and Legal History New York: Oxford University Press (1962) 73.

4. Ibid. 85-91.

5. Ibid. 156-57.

6. Ibid. 167-68.

7. "We may conclude that a parliament under Edward I was flexible in function, composition and organization. . . . It dispensed justice, discussed politics, legislated, and consented to taxation." Lyon, op. cit. 430.

8. Lovell op. cit. 168, 144-47.

9. Notably C. Peter Magrath, Elmer E. Cornwell, Jr., and Jay S. Goodman American Democracy Second Edition New York: Macmillan (1973) 428.

10. Brian Chapman The Profession of Government: The Public Service in Europe London: Allen and Unwin (1959) 48.

11. Woodrow Wilson "The Study of Administration" 2 Political Science Quarterly (1887) 197-222 at 218.

12. See chapter "The Communication Function" Gabriel A. Almond and G. Bingham Powell, Jr., Comparative Politics: A Developmental Approach Boston: Little, Brown (1966) 164-89.

13. Edmund S. Morgan The Birth of the Republic - 1763 - 1789. Chicago: University of Chicago Press (1956) 124.

14. Ibid. 125. Also: "The creation of a responsible staff of civil servants by the Confederation government is an almost unknown story. These men carried on the work of the departments of war, foreign affairs, finance and the post office in season and out. Many of them continued to be employed after 1789." Merrill Jensen The New Nation: A History of the United States during the Confederation, 1781-1789 New York: Knopf (1950) 360.

15. Jensen op. cit. 360 and Leonard D. White The Federalists: A Study in Administrative History New York: Macmillan (1948) 309.

16. The Department of Health Education and Welfare was the subject of Reorganization Plan 1 of 1953 but both houses of Congress specifically approved the departmentalization before the effective date of the Plan.

17. See generally David H. Rosenbloom Federal Service and the Constitution Ithaca, N.Y.: Cornell Unviersity Press (1971).

18. Wilfred E. Binkley President and Congress New York: Knopf (1947) 34, 39, 45.

19. Louis S. Loeb and Daniel M. Berman American Politics: Crisis and Challenge New York: Macmillan (1975) 237.

20. 1977 Congressional Directory 95th Cong. 1st. Sess. Washington: United States Government Printing Office (1977) 250-61, 276-97.

21. Richard E. Neustadt "Politicians and Bureaucrats" David B. Truman (Ed.) The American Assembly: The Congress and America's Future Second Edition Englewood Cliffs, N.J.: Prentice-Hall (1973) 118-40 at 119.

22. Ibid. 119, 120.

23. Milton C. Cummings and David Wise Democracy Under Pressure: An Introduction to the American Political System Third Edition New York: Harcourt Brace Jovanovich (1977) 461-63; David C. Saffell The Politics of American National Government Second Edition Cambridge, Mass. Winthrop (1975) 226.

24. Kenneth Prewitt and Sidney Verba An Introduction to American Government New York: Harper and Row (1974) 441.

25. Saffell op. cit. 224; Richard A. Watson Promise and Performance of American Democracy New York: John Wiley and Sons (1975) 334-38.

26. Walter F. Murphy and Michael N. Danielson Robert K. Carr and Marver H. Bernstein's American Democracy Eight Edition Hinsdale, Ill.: Dryden Press (1977) 293.

27. Clem Miller Member of the House New York: Scribners (1962) 110; see Neustadt op. cit. (fn 21) 119. Peter Woll and Robert Binstock America's Political System New York: Random House (1975) 309.

28. The Convention adopted the states as the units of apportionment even for Representatives. An 1842 statute made the single-member district plan nation wide. Joseph P. Harris Congress and the Legislative Process Second Edition New York: McGraw-Hill (1972) 55. District representation is now so much a part of our political beliefs that many people probably consider it to be a constitutional requirement.

29. Notes of Debates in the Federal Convention of 1787 Reported by James Madison New York: W. W. Norton (1969) 73-77, 82-87, 185-87, 193-97. Further references to debates reported in this edition of the Journal will be by date of the particular debate.

30. David Hume "Of Parties in General" Charles W. Hendel (Ed.) David Hume's Political Essays Indianapolis: Bobbs-Merrill (1953) 77-84.

31. Jean Jacques Rousseau The Social Contract New York: Hafner (1947) II, 3, pp. 26-27.

32. Michael Weinstein Philosophy, Theory and Method in Contemporary Political Thought Glenview, Ill. Scott, Foresman, (1971) 105-16, 156-75, 211-16; Edward McNall Burns Ideas in Conflict: The Political Theories of the Contemporary World New York: W. W. Norton (1960) 74-106, 111-20, 387-423, 426-59, 514-38, 543-64.

33. "The group model of policy formation suggests that interest groups are the focal point of the policy process, subsuming all of the legitimate political interests of the community." Peter Woll Public Policy Cambridge, Mass.: Winthrop (1974) 53. The development of a legitimizing ideology for special interest group process included the articulation of

such concepts as "polyarchal democracy," Robert A. Dahl A Preface to Democratic Theory Chicago: University of Chicago Press (1956) 63-89; and Robert A. Dahl Pluralist Democracy in the United States: Conflict and Consent Chicago: Rand McNally (1967) 22-24, 41.

34. The controversy extends into the teaching of the basic course in American national government. Some of the newer texts stress the elitist character of the special interest-group-governmental system, See Thomas R. Dye and L. Harmon Ziegler The Irony of Democracy: An Uncommon Introduction to American Politics Third Edition North Scituate, Mass.: Duxbury (1975); Michael Parenti Democracy for the Few New York: St. Martin's (1974); and Kenneth M. Dolbeare and Murray J. Edelman American Politics: Policies, Power and Change Second Edition, Lexington, Mass.: D. C. Heath (1074) This last includes governmental institutions in "The Integrated Economic-Political System." Older texts tend to take a neutral position while describing the elitist and pluralists positions, see William Ebenstein, C. Herman Pritchett, Henry A. Turner and Dean Mann American Democracy in World Perspective Fourth Edition New York: Harper and Row (1976) 6. One comparatively new text presents a third "model" that is "many-sided like the pluralist image, but relatively frozen in structure like the elitist model." Groups differ according to extent of internal participation. Olson and Meyer op. cit. (fn 1) 176-77. The idea that governments are essentially elitist was asserted at the turn of the century by European sociologists, Vilfredo Pareto, Gaetano Mosca and Roberto Michels. See Burns op. cit. (fn. 32) 76-88 and Weinstein op. cit. 32, 33, 104-26.

35. See for instance Thomas R. Dye, Lee S. Greene and George S. Parthemos American Government: Theory, Structure and Process Second Edition, Belmont, Calif.: Duxbury (1972) 179.

36. Watson op. cit. 194; Prewitt and Verba op. cit. 225-26; Walter E. Volkomer American Government Brief Edition, Englewood Cliffs, N.J.: Prentice-Hall (1975) 226-27; Cummings and Wise op. cit. 201.

37. George Goodwin, Jr., "Subcommittees: The Miniature Legislatures of Congress," 56 American Political Science Review (Sept. 1962) 596-604.

38. Neustadt op. cit. (fn 21) 120.

39. Carr, Bernstein, Murphy and Danielson op. cit. 260, 265-66, 293-301; Ebenstein, Pritchett, Turner and Mann op. cit. 310-11; James MacGregor Burns and J. W. Peltason with Thomas E. Cronin Government by the People Ninth Edition, Englewood Cliffs, N.J.: Prentice-Hall (1975) 379-80; Robert L. Keighton with Martin P. Sutton One Nation Lexington, Mass.: D. C. Heath (1972) 263.

40. Watson op. cit. 338; Ebenstein, Pritchett, Turner and Mann op. cit. 319-320.

41. Saffell op. cit. 224.

42. The Code of Federal Regulations is reissued annually while the United States Code is reissued much less frequently.

43. Dushkin Contributors, Issac Krammick, Academic Editor. American Government '73 '74, Text Guildford Conn.: Dushkin Publishing (1973) 234.

44. Carr, Bernstein, Murphy and Danielson op. cit. 255; See also Louis W. Koenig Toward a Democracy New York: Harcourt Brace Jovanovich (1973) 271-72.

45. Watson op. cit. 315.

46. Loeb and Berman op. cit. 271.

47. Woll and Binstock op. cit. 392.

48. Stephen V. Monsma American Politics Third Edition Hinsdale, Ill.: Dryden (1976) 192-93.

49. Saffell op. cit. 295, quoting Professor Richard F. Fenno, Jr.

50. The New York Times Feb. 1, 1977, 18; Feb. 18, 1977, B6. A recent volume seeks a cabinet reconstituted to provide presidential advice. Stephen Hess, Organizing the Presidency Washington: The Brookings Institution (1976) 206-218.

51. Thomas E. Cronin The State of the Presidency Boston: Little, Brown (1975) 184.

52. Ibid. 183.

53. Richard E. Neustadt Presidential Power: The Politics of Leadership New York: John Wiley (1960) 156; (1976) 224.

54. Dale Vinyard The Presidency New York: Scribner's (1971) 116.

55. Louis C. Gawthrop Administrative Politics and Social Change New York: St. Martin's (1971) 23.

56. Harold Seidman Politics, Position and Power: The Dynamics of Federal Organization New York: Oxford University Press (1970) 100-101.

57. See Richard E. Fenno, Jr., "The Role of the Cabinet" Francis E. Rourke (Ed.) Bureaucratic Power in National Politics Second Edition Boston: Little, Brown (1972) 152-64 at 153, 155, 161.

58. Gawthrop op. cit. 24.

59. Louis W. Koenig Congress and the President Chicago: Scott, Foresman (1965) 93-94.

60. Saffell op. cit. 296.

61. Cummings and Wise op. cit. 422.

62. Louis C. Gawthrop Bureaucratic Behavior in the Executive Branch New York: The Free Press (1969) 81. The Carter administration "is perhaps the least hierarchical we have had since World War II." The New York Times, Editorial, December 19, 1977.

63. Peter Woll Public Policy Cambridge, Mass.: Winthrop (1974) 77, 186-90, 237-45.

64. Administrative Procedure Act 5 U.S. Code 551-59.

65. Kenneth Culp Davis Administrative Law and Government St. Paul, Minn.: West Publishing (1960) 11.

66. 2 United States Code 192.

67. Barenblatt v. United States 360 U.S. 178 (1959).

68. Martin Birnbach American Political Life Homewood, Ill.: Dorsey (1971) 290-94; Cummings and Wise op. cit. 463-65; Dye, Greene and Parthemos op. cit. 235-36; Karl A. Lamb The People, Maybe Second Edition North Scituate, Mass.: Duxbury (1974) 162, 204.

69. Lamb op. cit. 162; Burns and Peltason with Cronin op. cit. 380.

70. Marian D. Irish, James W. Prothro and Richard J. Richardson The Politics of American Democracy Sixth Edition Englewood Cliffs, N.J.: Prentice-Hall (1977) 293; Watson op. cit. 316.

71. Rowland Egger The President of the United States Second Edition New York: McGraw-Hill (1972) 45; Dorothy B. James The Contemporary Presidency Second Edition Indianapolis: Bobbs-Merrill (1974) 212; McGeorge Bundy The Strength of Government Cambridge, Mass.: Harvard University Press (1968) 37; Philippa Strum Presidential Power and American Democracy Pacific Palisades, Calif.: Goodyear (1972) 46; Erwin C. Hargrove The Power of the Modern Presidency Philadelphia: Temple University Press (1974) 237; Stephen K. Bailey Congress in the Seventies New York: St. Martin's (1970) 28.

72. See Appendix A: Items 2, 7, 26, 30 and 37.

73. See Appendix A: Items 12, 13, 16 and 25.

74. See Appendix A: Items 20, 39, 44, 47 and 57.

75. William L. Morrow Public Administration: Politics and the Political System New York: Random House (1975) 6.

76. "Bureaucracy-out-of-control" Charles M. Hardin Presidential Power and Accountability Chicago: University of Chicago Press (1974) 14; Woll, op. cit. (fn 63) 255; Cronin op. cit. (fn 51) 69; See also Appendix A: Items 3, 13, 24, 39, 51, 52 and 57.

77. For instance, Louis W. Koenig Toward A Democracy: An Introduction to American Government New York: Harcourt Brace Jovanovich (1973) 241-43.

78. See supra Specialized Representation.

79. See fn. 36, supra.

80. "The people have never been interested in choosing professional managers for President, and professional managers do not run for the office. The presidential selection system is designed to screen politicians, and politicians are rarely trained as managers. Presidents as politicians recognize that management questions--except perhaps calls for 'economizing'--have little political appeal and great political risk. What makes this particularly ironic is that the history of the modern presidency has been one of growing presidential involvement in management. . . . But one result of adding to the role of the President as manager is that he spends more and more time doing that which he does badly and, presumably, has less and less time to devote to matters that only the President can handle. In sum, the role of the President as manager has been distorted in theory and in recent practice, leading the President to become involved in tasks that can be performed better by others. . . . the primary presidential role is to make choices--choices that are ultimately political in nature. . . . the political process primarily concerns distribution, not production. It decides who gets how much of what is available, not how to make more available at less cost. A political process cannot be managed in the sense that a corporation is managed, for political decisions are judged according to their fairness, both in the way they are made and in their perceived effect." Stephen Hess Organizing the Presidency Washington, D.C.: The Brookings Institution (1976) 146, 147. "Americans look to their President to satisfy at least three sets of needs. First is the need for reassurance. . . . Beyond reassurance, people want a sense of progress and action. . . . Then people want a sense of legitimacy from and in the presidency. Again there is an apparant contradiction: he should be a master politician who is above politics. He should have a right to his place and a rightful way of

acting in it. The responsibility—even religiosity—of the office has to be protected by a man who presents himself as defender of the faith. There is more to this than dignity, though, more than an air of propriety. The President is expected to personify our betterness in an inspiring way, to express in what he does and is (not just what he says) a moral idealism which in much of the public mind, is the very opposite of 'politics'. James D. Barber "The Presidency: What Americans Want" The Center Magazine (Jan/Feb 1971) 2-6; reprinted Stanley Bach and George T. Sulzner Perspectives on the Presidency Lexington, Mass.: D. C. Heath (1974) 144-51 at 145.

CONCLUSION

This book has examined the constitutional function of the persistent separation of presidential and administrative forces in the specialized operations of the United States government. The inquiry is pertinent because, in the comprehensive explanations by political scientists of the American national government, there tends to be, on the one hand, much unsystematic recognition of a perdurable division within the formal executive branch and, on the other hand, firm adherence to an ideological model of only legislative, executive and judicial powers.

The short initial chapter reviewed the extent to which political science specialists and generalists recognize the pragmatic, horizontal separation of executive officials. The review focused upon the differentiation of noncareer and career appointees and upon the centricity of subdepartmental units. It also explained that the permanence of the presidential-administrative separation derives from various factors. These include the White House concentration upon public relations and upon a few selected headline issues, the wide scope of specialized government, the multiplicity of congressional-administrative relationships, the demands of "the rule of law" in governmental operations, and, most definitely of all, the inevitable difference between the short tenure of the presidential contingents and the career orientation of the thousands of specialized administrators appointed under the Civil Service or other merit system.

The first of the main chapters on the principles of constitutional distribution developed a number of ideas concerning the clauses vesting legislative, executive and judicial powers in Congress, a president and courts, respectively. One such idea is that the clause vesting executive power, when interpreted in conjunction with the companion clauses, suggests that the presidential function is to execute the laws made by Congress. Thus, it is a restricted basis of authority. The broader bases of presidential legal power are the specific constitutional grants, the statutory enactments, and the inherent character of the presidency. Moreover, the specialized character of much governmental activity means that execution of laws often falls directly upon operating subunits headed by career minded administrators. They determine much policy by non-criminal legislation and non-criminal adjudication. The White House forces devote themselves to many functions which seem more important than management of the administrative units. These include headline crises, diplomatic relations, program development, public relations, and maintenance of the presidential image. This body of functions is sufficient to make the presidential establishment a coordinate branch of government apart from the law-executing administrative branch.

The vesting clauses form a three-branch-separate-function pattern of government, in which there is a one-to-one correspondence between three functions--legislative, executive and judicial--and three separate institutions. That scheme is ideologically attractive but it seems peculiarly relevant to criminal law processes. Separation of these legal procedures developed to keep chief executives and elected assemblies from conducting criminal trials. Government now involves a much larger portion of non-criminal processes, such as civil regulation and development of various areas of the socio-economic system. In the non-criminal fields, there are many allocations which do not fit the three-branch-three-function model. Hence we need to distinguish the separation of functions from the separation of institutions. For the prevention of undue concentration, the separation of institutions is only a necessary preliminary. Final sufficiency depends upon the functional arrangement. Unless there is an established interdependence, such as there is in the three major criminal law processes, or a constitutionally prescribed sharing, such as there is in the enactment of statutes, the adoption of treaties, or the appointment of judges, functional separation may not serve to restrain abuse of power. Foreign affairs and national security are the areas in which one institution, usually the presidency, is likely to claim that separation of institutions justifies independence of functions. The Korean and Vietnam wars are prime examples. Those events also show the importance of checks and balances by other branches.

The second principal chapter examined the mixed power distribution in the main body of the Constitution. That pattern embraces checks and balances and shared functions. The foremost example is the inter-relationship of the president and the houses of Congress in various functions. The mixed power principle may be as broad as the Constitution. It can encompass the three-branch-separate-function doctrine in its proper realm, that is, in the criminal law field, where legislative, executive and judicial processes have an established interdependence. The mixed-power concept can be an ideal as well as a fact because its essential foundation is the psychological imperative of checking power with power. Separation of powers may or may not be an effective restraint; the answer is in the extent to which separate functions check each other. The separate power concept may give a false impression by suggesting the propriety of functional independence whereas the mixed power principle indicates the need of mutual counteraction.

The final chapter placed the constitutional legitimacy of administrative offices, bureaus, departments and agencies, upon inherent necessity and upon the express power of Congress to enact laws "necessary and proper for carrying into Execution" the powers of the government and of "any department or officer thereof." Congress determines the existence, authority, appropriations and other aspects of the administrative units. There is a multiplicity of particularized relationships between the subunits of the congressional and administrative realms. Specialized execution manifests mixed power constitutionalism in a number of ways. The administrative branch shares legislative power with Congress, adjudicative

104

power with the courts, and executive powers with the presidential establishment. Logically and practically, specialized administrators are dependent upon and responsive to Congress and the courts as well as to the executive heads. Responsibility to all three tends to facilitate independence of each and all.

The administrative process at times may combine legislative, executive and judicial actions, but subject particularization entails an expanded operation of checks and balances. It extends institutional separation into the subunit levels of the different branches. It reduces the authority of any single unit and it often gives rise to counterbalance. For instance, the different systems for regulation—transportation, communication, trade, agriculture, energy, labor relations and so on—have restrictive force upon each other. Subject particularization also makes for fragmentation of congressional-administrative relationships, and of interest group pressures. Moreover, as some political scientists have pointed out, the bureaucracy has the potential value of being a check upon the presidency and upon congressional units, if they stray beyond proper limits.

We are apt to assume that the president and the members of Congress control the appointed officials. But they give priority to the demands of political prestige and the forthcoming elections. In fact, the political competition between them absorbs much of their time. Moreover, their efforts to direct the administrators are mainly in response to pressures from constituents. Accordingly, the primary issue is not whether the president or Capitol Hill should control the bureaucracy, but rather how the "general public" can help them in the comprehensive task of making the specialized executives responsible and responsive to proper interests and ideals. That would seem to require direct relationships between the concerned publics and the administrators because there is a substantial area, flexible in scope and identify, in which the administrative branch operates with much independence of any other branch.

Many interest groups now include direct relationships with appointed executives in their efforts to control particular operating policies. But those groups protect little more than a third of the public. The development of broader participation entails greater awareness of the power of specialized administrators. These last are difficult to visualize and to conceptualize because of their multiplicity and their low visibility. They lack the newsworthy quality of the president and the leading figures of the White House, Congress and the Supreme Court. Thus, there is educational challenge in the recognition of the presidential-administrative separation.

Wider public participation in the special and general interest groups, which seek to guide specialized administrators, could mean that the top levels of departmental officials and also the Executive Office leaders, have more time and energy for general and higher functions, such as more comprehensive programs and projects. That in turn would tend to elevate the role of the presidency. Thus, the separation of presidential government from particularized administration raises the potential quality of White House actions.

The old maxim that we need singularity of responsibility has not done well during the past dozen years. It did not prevent the Vietnam escalation, the Watergate misdirection, or the Nixon pardon. There is only hollow satisfaction in knowing the one to blame. Interdependence of action is more likely to prevent mistakes of judgment.

Americans need not be disturbed constitutionally by the fact that the pattern of four coordinate branches—congressional, executive, judicial and administrative—is descriptive of the specialized operations of the government at least as much and probably more than the better known three branch model. The development of the presidency and the bureaucracy in separate directions is a modern adaptation of the underlying principles of constitutional distribution and aids the attainment of their objectives. But Americans may need to be disturbed politically if they concentrate their attention upon the elected officials, and do not also enter the processes of direct pressure upon the appointed executives in the less visible and more specialized realms of government. The extent of democratic or public control of the governmental operations is not measured merely by the degree of participation in the nomination and election of the president and the members of Congress. It is also measured by the extent of active involvement in the processes of exerting direct guidance and restraint upon the specialized administrators.

The four-branch-mixed-power pattern is less a rejection than a refinement of the three-branch-separate-function model. It takes into account the developments with respect to both the public-image-presidency and the specialized-career-bureaucracy. The four branch concept can serve to remind us both of what is happening in the government and how we must proceed to exert control upon the multiple centers of policy formulation. Recognition of the continuing separation of presidential-administrative forces and of its constitutional function is essential to a full understanding of the practice and the theory of American national government.

APPENDIX A
RELATIONSHIP OF THE PRESIDENCY
AND THE ADMINISTRATIVE BUREAUCRACY

Most of the more than fifty political science textbooks for the introductory university course in American national government indicate that to some appreciable degree the presidency lacks full control of the executive branch. Set forth below are relevant excerpts from such volumes in alphabetical order. The various statements differ in their views of the scope and intensity of the division within the formal executive system, but most of the excerpts suggest that the administrative bureaucracy responds to a mixture of forces, such as congressional committees and subcommittees, the courts, special interest groups, and professional standards, as well as the officials of the presidential contingent.

1. The root of what makes the federal system so conflict-ridden is that the Founding Fathers provided it with four legislative branches . . . . Each of these branches, the Presidency, the courts, the Congress, and the bureaucracy, has an important policy-making role. Each also is different in composition and in the assumptions it holds. Each has its own set of exclusive legal powers, its own independent methods of organization, its own pattern of recruitment, and its own separate, special constituencies. . . . The legal powers the President holds thus do not make him the inevitable winner in a conflict over policy, but they insure that usually in one term and almost certainly if he serves two terms, no one else can win without his consent. Inevitably, to get action over the long run, the other branches know that they have to strike a bargain with the presidential office. Thus compromise and cooperation and also direction are forced upon the system. Charles R. Adrian and Charles Press American Politics Reappraised: The Enchantment of Camelot Dispelled New York: McGraw-Hill (1974) 160, 163.

2. The close relationships frequently found among congressional committees, private and public interest groups, and influential administrative agencies reinforce the decentralizationist forces, especially in face of conflicting presidential or party claims. Donald T. Allensworth The U.S. Government in Action: Policy and Structure Pacific Palisades, Calif.: Goodyear (1972) 57.

3. We feel that the bureaucracy, contrary to the intentions of the founders, has become a fourth branch of government with a life all its own. . . . The bureaucracy flaunts constitutive law in much the same way

107

and to much the same extent as do the other branches. Therein lies the illegitimacy of the administrative state as it is practiced in America. For it is part and parcel of the ever-growing illegitimacy of all government in America. Theodore L. Becker American Government--Past--Present--Future Boston: Allyn and Bacon (1976) 272, 292.

4. What is required of bureaucrats is not that they will "obey the president" (who is not their immediate superior anyway), but rather that they will conform to the rules and expectations of their specified roles. Roderick A. Bell and David V. Edwards American Government: The Facts Reorganized Morristown, N.J. General Learning Co. (1974) 146.

5. With unrivalled knowledge from the departments and agencies at his fingertips, the President can formulate plans and project policy. Strange as it might seem, however, many departments and agencies do not owe their primary loyalty to the President. Some agencies have achieved a semi-autonomous existence which they are intent on preserving. . . . They are oriented more toward their clienteles than toward the chief executive (often with the support of Congress), for their chiefs know that their continued prosperity depends more on the recipients of their services than on Presidents who come and go. To obtain innovating ideas and thoroughgoing reforms, to secure confidential counsel, the President can rely little on the regular departments and agencies. Martin Birnbach American Political Life: An Introduction to United States Government Homewood, Ill.: Dorsey Press (1971) 297-98.

6. At every level of American government--indeed, in most governments of the world--the strings of power are pulled by enterprises variously called the "administration," the "fourth branch of government," and the "bureaucracy." Blanche D. Blank American Government and Politics: A Critical Introduction Chicago: Aldine (1973) 126.

7. Administrators often have more bargaining and political alliance-building skills than the elected and appointed officials to whom they report. In one sense, agency leaders are at the center of action in Washington. . . . Some of the agencies have so much support among interest groups and Congress that a president would hesitate to move against them. James MacGregor Burns and J. W. Peltason with Thomas E. Cronin Government by the People Ninth Edition Englewood Cliffs, N.J.: Prentice-Hall (1975) 482, 491.

8. The Constitution established only three branches of government, but the demands of a modern industrialized society have combined with a variety of political forces to establish a "fourth branch" of government--the bureaucracy. David A. Caputo Politics and Public Policy in America: An Introduction Philadelphia: J. B. Lippincott (1974) 105.

9. A crucial test of our modern democratic society is the maintenance of an effective bureaucracy while preserving popular control. Presently, the power is definitely on the side of the mighty bureaucracy.

John P. Carney Nation of Change: The American Democratic System
Second Edition San Francisco, Calif.: Canfield Press (1975) 173.

10. One of the basic facts of life with which a President or any other
executive official must come to terms is that the federal bureaucracy is
not a monolithic unit. And it certainly is not neat. It operates much more
like the two decentralized political parties than like a disciplined semi-
military organization. The analogy to the two political parties is no
accident. . . . Legislators, drawing the vital juices of re-election from
state and local constituencies, work hard to ensure that the bureaucracy
will be less the creature of the President's will and more the benefactor of
their constituents. The armed forces may be an exception to this rule in
actual combat, but not the way in which the various services purchase
supplies or build bases. Walter F. Murphy and Michael N. Danielson
Robert K. Carr and Marver H. Bernstein's American Democracy Eight
Edition Hinsdale, Ill.: Dryden Press (1977) 364.

11. Although Cabinet members or bureaucrats are rarely insubordinate to the President in the face of a direct command, such direct
commands are rare. The President is too busy to confront every situation
in which his preferences are being frustrated. C. R. M. Books American
Government Today Del Mar, Calif.: Ziff-Davis (1974) 293.

12. Despite his vast constitutional and extraconstitutional powers,
the President is sometimes as much a victim of bureaucratic inertia as
anyone else. . . . In theory, Presidents make policy and bureaucrats carry
it out. In fact, officials often play a major role in policy formation. In
large part, this is because Presidents rely on bureaucratic *expertise*
in making their policy decisions. Milton C. Cummings, Jr., and David Wise
Democracy Under Pressure: An Introduction to the American Political
System Third Edition New York: Harcourt Brace Jovanovich (1977) 362,
428-29.

13. Congress, the Presidency, and the judiciary govern, but they
cannot do the actual daily work of governing. . . . Most public policy in
fact is carried out through the administrative system. Congress, the
Presidency, and the courts are in a sense small groups of men clustered
among this behemoth, trying to guide it, train it, prod it this way and that.
Martin Diamond, Winston Mills Fisk and Herbert Garfinkel The Democratic Republic: An Introduction to American National Government Second
Edition, Chicago: Rand McNally (1970) 249-50.

14. Major constraints on presidential power flow from such sources
as the Congress, the influence of forthcoming elections, and national or
international events. But the greatest continuing constraint of all is the
bureaucracy. Kenneth M. Dolbeare and Murray J. Edelman American
Politics: Policies, Power and Change, Second Edition, Lexington, Mass.:
D. C. Heath (1974) 316.

15. . . . there is a clear division within the executive between presidential government, composed of the thin layer of presidential appointees

in the White House and at the top of each department, and the permanent government made up of civil servants who see the presidents come and go. These professional bureaucrats feel no special loyalty to the White House. Dushkin contributors, Issac Krammick, Academic Editor American Government '73 '74 Text Guilford, Conn.: Dushkin (1973) 142.

16. In the American system of government, control of the bureaucracy is exercised by Congress, the chief executive, the courts, and, to some extent, pressure groups. Thomas R. Dye, Lee S. Greene, and George S. Parthemos, American Government: Theory, Structure, and Process Second Edition Belmont, Calif.: Duxbury (1972) 352.

17. The president is the first among equals of America's elites. His real power depends not on his formal authority but on his abilities of persuasion. Moreover, the president must still function within the established elite system. Thomas R. Dye and L. Harmon Ziegler The Irony of Democracy: An Uncommon Introduction to American Politics Third Edition North Scituate, Mass.: Duxbury (1975) 318.

18. In the constitutional sense, the President has authority over, and is responsible for, the activity of every member of the executive establishment. When he knows what he wants, when his principal aides and executives are in agreement, and when he exercises the full authority of his office, undoubtedly he can have his way. Unfortunately, he is but a single man, and even though his reach is much extended by his personal aides, the Office of Management and Budget, and the National Security Council, he cannot commit himself to more than a fraction of the public business. He must rely on the judgment and loyalty of his administrative subordinates, and this is often risky business, because Cabinet and sub-Cabinet officers often have their own clienteles and may be responsive to influences other than the President's. William C. Ebenstein, C. Herman Pritchett, Henry A. Turner and Dean Mann American Democracy in World Perspective Fourth Edition New York: Harper and Row (1976) 370-71.

19. Although the Constitution says "the executive power shall be vested in a President," and hierarchy appears to be pyramidal, the President is not in full command of Federal administration. . . . President Nixon went farther than other Presidents in trying to overcome this handicap by placing persons of demonstrated loyalty to him and his key aides on the staffs of certain departments and agencies with the expectation that communication would take place directly with them rather than through their superiors as is normally done. This practice compounded the President's difficulties by causing suspicion and resentment among those officially charged with responsibility for running their departments and agencies. John H. Ferguson and Dean E. McHenry The American Federal Government Thirteenth Edition New York: McGraw-Hill (1977) 286.

20. From time to time any branch of government takes on some of the attributes of other branches. Nonetheless, we have in the federal departments and agencies an enormous aggregation of decision-making

authority. Clearly there is power here—enough to suggest that the federal bureaucracy has become a fourth branch of government with many of the characteristics of the three constitutionally established branches. Leonard Freedman Power and Politics in America Second Edition North Scituate, Mass.: Duxbury (1974) 226.

21. The president is *only* the principal among several million decision makers in the executive branch . . . each is nonetheless as much of a human being as the president with respect to his basic processes of choice. Ralph M. Goldman Behavioral Perspectives on American Politics. Homewood, Ill.: Dorsey (1973) 168.

22. If we wanted to find the bulk of federal "law" that governs the country today, we would go not to the Statutes at Large passed by Congress, but rather to the Federal Register, which contains the executive orders, directives, rules, and regulations adopted by the national administration. Congress enacts general policies, but more and more it leaves the details of regulation to the administrative agencies. Not only the independent regulatory commissions but also the executive departments issue regulations with the force of law. . . . Today a hundred or more federal agencies make rules that are legally binding. Marian D. Irish, James W. Prothro and Richard J. Richardson The Politics of American Democracy Sixth Edition Englewood Cliffs, N.J.: Prentice-Hall (1977) 353-54.

23. Centrifugal forces found in all departments challenge even the most resourceful leadership seeking to establish central direction over the affairs of the bureaucracy. . . . Competition of bureaus for new activities and congressional appropriations, as well as conflicting purposes of bureaus, work against departmental unity. . . . Administration in the federal government is complicated by the geographic dispersal of its activities, despite the marvels of jet age travel and electronic communication. With 90 percent of the federal bureaucracy working outside Washington, D.C., there are inherent difficulties in articulating the constitutent parts of the scattered administraiton. Claudius O. Johnson, Daniel M. Ogden, Jr., H. Paul Castleberry and Thor Swanson American National Government Seventh Edition New York: Thomas Y. Crowell (1970) 331.

24. The bureaucracy has become a "fourth branch of government" not only because it was able to respond to the needs of public policy but also out of the inability of other branches of government to meet these needs. Harvey M. Karlen The Pattern of American Government Second Edition Beverly Hills, Calif.: Glencoe Press (1975) 275.

25. Control of administration is exercised by the presidency, by the Congress, and by the courts. Theoretically, it is the president by way of his departments who has the final authority in the area of internal control, but as has been seen, there are varying degrees of departmental control.

Robert L. Keighton with Martin P. Sutton <u>One</u> <u>Nation:</u> <u>An</u> <u>American</u> <u>Government</u> <u>Text</u> <u>with</u> <u>Readings</u> Lexington, Mass.: D. C. Heath (1972) 233-34.

26. Although he presumably presides over the executive branch, the President is far from being its master. Congress, for one, is a potent presence. Acts of Congress determine what the departments do and give them authority to do it. . . . Often congressional surveillance is directed to keeping the agency within bounds desired by interest groups, however different they are from the President's view of the agency's mission. . . . On occasion, the courts, may thwart the President when he asserts administrative leadership. . . . The bureaucracy itself can resist the President. It can delay and dilute what he wants done. Louis W. Koenig <u>Toward a</u> <u>Democracy:</u> <u>A</u> <u>Brief</u> <u>Introduction</u> to <u>American</u> <u>Government</u> New York: Harcourt Brace Jovanovich (1973) 228, 229, 230.

27. For the President who means to change policy, the bureaucracy can be a source of tension and friction. The giant bureaucracy is committed to doing things the way they have been done in the past. Louis W. Koenig, Glendon Schubert, Lloyd D. Musolf, Laurence I. Radway, and John Fenton <u>American</u> <u>National</u> <u>Government:</u> <u>Policy</u> <u>and</u> <u>Politics</u> Glenview, Ill.: Scott, Foresman (1971), 311.

28. The federal bureaucracy . . . is made up of persons and organizations separate from the president who share his executive authority. . . . Governmental agencies normally develop sources of support in Congress, and in the nation, that are independent of the president. Karl A. Lamb <u>The</u> <u>People,</u> <u>Maybe</u> Second Edition, North Scituate, Mass.: Duxbury (1974), 108, 109.

29. True enough, the President is the Chief Administrator in the United States and generally held accountable for the whole executive establishment. But it must be realized that he has little direct control over much of the bureaucracy, for they are in practice "independent" of him in many ways. Erwin L. Levine and Elmer E. Cornwell, Jr., <u>An</u> <u>Introduction</u> to <u>American</u> <u>Government</u> Second Edition New York: Macmillan (1972) 164.

30. In addition to organizational inertia and agency pressure on Congress, the President must struggle for control with other enemies as well. Highly placed bureaucracies, congressmen, and pressure groups all occasionally compete with him for control of administrative agencies. John C. Livingston and Robert G. Thompson <u>The</u> <u>Consent</u> <u>of</u> <u>the</u> <u>Governed</u> Third Edition: New York: Macmillan (1971) 408.

31. The existence of coalitions and subsystems that cut across institutional lines means that no president, however resourceful, is ever truly the master of his own house. The centrifugal pressures within the bureaucracy mean that the president often is chief executive and chief administrator in name only. Louis Loeb and Daniel M. Berman <u>American</u> <u>Politics:</u> <u>Crisis</u> <u>and</u> <u>Challenge</u> New York: Macmillan (1975) 273.

32. The enormous stature and energy of a single chief executive, coupled with the constitutional authority of the office of president, ought to be adequate to control bureaucracy. The trouble is that the president, like a modern prime minister or military dictator, is confronted by an almost equal formal authority held by the bureaucracy. The formal position of the bureaucracy is not explicitly granted by the Constitution, but it does have a statutory, judicial, professional, cultural, and historical basis. There will never be sufficient presidential power to cope with these large institutions, because there can never be a sufficient amount of formal authority plus informal power in the presidency to overblance the position of the bureaucracies. Theodore J. Lowi American Government: Incomplete Conquest Hinsdale, Ill.: Dryden Press (1976) 507.

33. Ironically, the specter of a powerful and relatively autonomous Fourth Branch of government in the form of a bureaucracy is the result of the Founders' fear of unrestrained power. For it is the very constitutional fragmentation of power designed by the Founders to prevent tyranny that has made the bureaucracy incompletely controlled by any of the traditional branches of government. Fred R. Mabbutt and Gerald J. Ghelfi The Troubled Republic: American Government, Its Principles and Problems New York: John Wiley and Sons (1974) 170.

34. . . . administrative structures have evolved in America, responding far less to textbook definitions and patterns than to the traditions and folkways of an essentially antibureaucratic political culture. Yet these forms of resistance could not halt but only deflect the development of the labyrinth of forms and euphemisms that today make up the gigantic "fourth branch" of the American federal government. C. Peter Magrath, Elmer E. Cornwell, Jr., and Jay S. Goodman The American Democracy Second Edition New York: Macmillan (1973) 444.

35. Though the line organizations of the departments and the executive agencies, and the staff organizations of the Executive Office of the President can be neatly drawn on an organizational chart, the President in actuality is the head of an executive two-headed Hydra, which is often working at cross-purposes. J. Keith Melville The American Democratic System New York: Dodd, Mead (1975) 172.

36. Whether and how bureaucrats respond to presidential directives often of necessity goes unnoticed by the President and his aides because of their limited time and the sheer size of the bureaucracies. Months may pass before the White House learns that a directive has not been carried out. Bureaucrats are also frequently able to avoid following presidential wishes if—as is often the case—they have strong supporters in Congress or in outside client groups. Stephen V. Monsma American Politics Third Edition Hinsdale, Ill.: Dryden (1976) 275.

37. Although they are under the direction of the president, administrative agencies commonly have extremely cozy relations with certain powerful congressional leaders and with the committees with which they

must regularly deal. . . . Robert L. Morlan American Government: Policy and Process Second Edition Boston: Houghton Mifflin (1975) 201.

38. No treatment of the operations and functions of the federal government's established institutions would be complete without devoting considerable attention to the "fourth branch." Although not specifically established by the Constitution, the Founders *assumed* that some type of administrative structure would evolve, and that it would be officially under the control of the President. We have already noted that such control is necessarily incomplete, that the President must persuade bureaucracies to do what he wants just as he tries to persuade Congressmen. The bureaucracy is very much an important political force independent of the President. Robert E. O'Connor and Thomas G. Ingersoll The Politics of Structure: The Essential Features of American National Government North Scituate, Mass.: Duxbury (1975) 141.

39. Congress and the President have been in continuous contention for control of the bureaucracy, and one effect has been to give the agencies the opportunity to play one off against the other, thus remaining largely self-controlled. David J. Olson and Philip Meyer To Keep the Republic: Governing the United States in its Third Century New York: McGraw-Hill (1975) 392.

40. This national bureaucracy of ours, with its three million civilian employees, has been called the fourth branch of government. Some people think it has grown into the most powerful branch of all, with perhaps the most profound effect upon the daily lives of Americans. Dennis J. Palumbo American Politics New York: Appleton-Century-Crofts (1973) 271.

41. The political process does not end with the passage of a bill but continues with equal or even greater intensity at the administrative level, albeit in more covert fashion. Michael Parenti Democracy for the Few New York: St. Martin's (1974) 232.

42. We talk of the executive vs. Congress as if they were two individuals in conflict. In fact, neither the executive nor Congress is a single entity. The executive branch in particular is a huge, sprawling bureaucracy. Within the executive branch are many other independent power centers. . . . The President is constitutionally in charge of the executive branch, but in practice he is lucky to know what is taking place in even a tiny part of it. Kenneth Prewitt and Sidney Verba An Introduction to American Government Second Edition New York: Harper and Row (1976) 372, 373.

43. The sheer incapacity to deal with agencies legally subordinate to the White House is a significant check on Presidential powers. The organizational tools available to the President, his own staff and cabinet, are not sufficient to the challenge of imposing Presidential control over the bureaucracy. Kenneth Prewitt and Sidney Verba Principles of American Government New York: Harper and Row (1975) 297.

44. Virtually every agency in the federal bureaucracy has an identifiable clientele in the private sector. . . . Clients are important to agencies because they can both give needed support as the agencies seek funds and personnel from the Office of Management and Budget and from Congress, and they can also withhold that support. In addition, they can often provide agency officials with valuable feedback on how well the programs of the agency are being administered from the point of view of the recipients. Randall B. Ripley American National Government and Public Policy New York: Free Press (1974) 155-56.

45. Americans overrate the President's political power as often as they underrate the professional bureaucracy as a powerful element of American national government. Robert S. Ross American National Government: An Introduction to Political Institutions, Second Edition Chicago: Rand McNally (1976) 133.

46. In any administration most of the bureaucrats were on the job before the president took office and they will still be around after he leaves. Typically the new president comes to Washington filled with ideas and quickly runs into the leaders of the permanent government who are firmly placed in their private domains and resist proposals for change made by what they see as a temporary intruder in their midst. More often than not it is the president who backs away from the confrontation and the bureaucrats are left to carry on as usual. David C. Saffell The Politics of American Government Second Edition Cambridge, Mass.: Winthrop (1975) 288, 289.

47. Bureaucratic agencies have an immense impact on U.S. public policy. In the area of national security, for example, bureaucrats in the Central Intelligence Agency, the military, and the State Department have initiated and directed American foreign policy. They shaped President Truman's Greek-Turkish aid program in 1946-47, the Marshall Plan for economic assistance to Europe, the NATO alliance in 1949, and the war effort in Vietnam. It was largely the bureaucrats who persuaded Congress to endorse and support their policies with funds and political rhetoric. Publication of the Pentagon Papers in 1971, for example, revealed that from the very beginning of the American involvement in Vietnam, the bureaucratic agencies shaped and executed policy decisions. . . . Demonstrators against the war in Vietnam sensed more clearly the role bureaucratic agencies played in the war effort. It was no accident, therefore, that so much of the protest campaign against Vietnam policy was directed at the Pentagon. That vast house of bureaucracy was, in fact, where policy was made. Robert H. Salisbury Governing America: Public Choice and Political Action New York: Appleton-Century-Crofts (1973) 302.

48. Bureaucracies have become a fourth branch of government. . . . The bureaucracy is not accountable to the public at large. It is in a position to regulate itself as an autonomous institution. There is ambiguity of responsibility regarding its control. The entrenched institutional interests of the bureaucracy threaten any political system

which prides itself on responsiveness to, and control by, the people. In the American system, the power of the bureaucracy has been limited and controlled primarily by the pluralistic nature of politics which is reflected in the bureaucratic structure. Sam C. Sarkesian and Krish Nanda Politics and Power: An Introduction to American Government New York: Alfred (1976) 367.

49. Popular mythology often exaggerates the President's powers and capabilities; there are many problems, both international and domestic, over which he has little control. The ironic contrast between the authority of the President and his actual capacity to shape policy is one of the great fascinations of American politics. The President is formally the Commander in Chief of the Armed Forces, though this does not mean that he controls the activities of all military personnel. All administrative officials are theoretically answerable to the President, but this does not guarantee that they will respond to his preferences and directives. Ira Sharkansky and Donald Van Meter Policy and Politics in American Governments New York: McGraw-Hill (1975) 241.

50. The President and his advisors simply do not have the time to determine whether his orders are being carried out, ignored, or resisted by federal departments and agencies. And when the President determines that an agency's head has sabotaged his policy, he may be unable to combat the agency without paying a high price to its clientele groups and congressional cohorts. Therefore, even a strong President ignores most agencies most of the time, hopes that federal agencies do not confront him with visible corruption, disloyalty, or mismanagement, and concentrates his energies on the few agencies and programs he wants to affect during his limited tenure. Ruth C. Silva, Edward Keynes, Hugh A. Bone, and David W. Adamany American Government: Democracy and Liberty in Balance New York: Knopf (1976) 341.

51. The ability of the bureaucracy to escape executive supervision additionally means that it is not subject to popular control, a major criterion of democracy. But bureaucracy seems inevitable, so ways must be found to limit its worst tendencies. The answer lies in developing more effective political leadership of the bureaucracies. Max J. Skidmore and Marshall Carter Wanke American Government: A Brief Introduction New York: St. Martin's (1974) 104.

52. There is no easy way for either voters or their elected officials to compel a vast bureaucracy to carry out its role in the public's interest. Random checks may be made and flagrant abuses may be investigated. But still the system is too large and too complex to be placed under constant watch. Thus we must rely to a great extent on the positive influence of our political culture. Its stress on the rule of law, on the importance of fair treatment, and on procedures for redress of grievances provides one method of checking the bureaucracy. Charles P. Sohner American Government and Politics Today Second Edition Glenview, Ill.: Scott, Foresman (1976) 297.

53. Although the President exercises a great deal of control over the bureaucracy through this White Houe staff, the Office of Management and Budget, and the cabinet, his influence is weakened by his need to rely on career executives or civil servants further down the line to promote and defend his policies. Often, these people have the political support of powerful interest groups and influential members of Congress, and may promote interests other than the President's. Walter E. Volkomer American Government Brief Edition Englewood Cliffs, N.J.: Prentice-Hall (1975) 441.

54. The ability of the late FBI Director J. Edgar Hoover and of former Selective Service Director Lewis Hershey to outlast a number of presidents is testimony to the power of agency heads to resist the most serious efforts of the president . . . . Stephen L. Wasby American Government and Politics New York: Scribners' (1973) 535.

55. Arthur Schlesinger reports in his biography of President Kennedy, A Thousand Days, that the resistance Kennedy encountered from executive officials was almost as great as the opposition of congressmen. Kennedy's difficulties were not peculiar to him alone. All Presidents have had similar experiences. Richard A. Watson Promise and Performance of American Democracy Second Edition John Wiley and Sons (1975) 406.

56. The federal bureaucracy is sufficiently large and independent of presidential control to constitute a fourth branch of government. Its basic units are the cabinet-level departments, each of which is sub-divided into bureaus. . . . Much federal administration is done indirectly through grants and contracts. Thus federal administration involves not only the federal bureaucracy but millions of state and local administrators and employees of private firms. . . . Because agencies are highly specialized but operate overlapping programs, the federal administration employs both hierarchical and lateral methods of coordination. Raymond E. Wolfinger, Martin Shapiro, and Fred I. Greenstein Dynamics of American Politics Englewood Cliffs, N.J.: Prentice-Hall (1976) 474.

57. A second major dilemma of our constitutional system is the fact that the bureaucracy as a fourth branch of government is not provided for by the Constitution. . . . Attempts to make the bureaucracy fit into the tripartite system of government have still not satisfied some political observers. As the bureaucracy has grown and become increasingly autonomous, it has been difficult to determine how the power of this administrative branch of government can be controlled. Peter Woll and Robert H. Binstock America's Political System Second Edition New York: Random House (1975) xviii, 370.

INDEX

Aberbach, Joel D., 77

Abuse of power, 27, 28, 55, 72, 73, 94, 104, 106

Adamany, David W., 116

Adams, John, 27, 57

Administrative adjudication, 7, 31, 40, 67, 91-96, 103 105

Administrative institutions, 6-9, 66, 80-82, 91, 95, 97

Administrative legislation, 7, 32-34, 47, 52, 89, 111

Administrative separation, 12, 67, 71-73, 93, 96, 97, 106; see also Bureaucracy

Adrian, Charles R., 107

Allensworth, Donald T., 107

Almond, Gabriel A., 75, 97

Appointing power, 37, 43, 66-67; Career appointees, 2, 5, 6, 10, 13-17, 72, 77, 91; Noncareer appointees, 2, 6, 15, 17, 18, 20, 22, 77, 90-91

Aristotle, 56, 76

Bach, Stanley, 18, 102

Bailey, Stephen K., 5, 101

Barber, James D., 21, 102

Becker, Theodore L., 108

Bell, Roderick A., 108

Berman, Daniel M., 76, 98, 100, 112

Bernstein, Marver H., 75, 98, 99, 100, 109

Bicameralism, 26, 37, 53-58, 60, 62-65, 84-85

Binkley, Wilfred E., 49, 98

Binstock, Robert H., 75, 98, 100, 117

Congressional branch, Delegation of powers, 32-34; Functional diversity, 34-35; Institutional separation, 43-48; Representational role, 62-65; Subunits, 6, 87-89

Congressional relationships, Administrative, 18-19, 33-35, 46, 49, 52, 65-68 91-93; Presidential, 35-39, 45-49, 61-68

Congressional veto on regulations, 33, 34, 50, 52

Conn, Paul H., 75

Constitutional principles, Administrative structures, 49, 65-67, 81-82, 97; Branch interdependence, 6, 49, 68-70; Checks and balances, 53, 58-59, 62, 70-73, 75; Congressional powers, 32-35, 52, 93; Distribution patterns, 2, 3, 23, 24, 53, 79; Institutional separation, 23, 40-48, 52, 104-106; Presidential powers, 31, 35-39; Representation, 62-65, 84 85; Separation of powers, 25, 28, 51; Vesting clauses, 23, 29, 30, 32, 46-48

Cornwell, Elmer E., Jr., 97, 112, 113

Corwin, Edward S., 77

Criminal law processes, Established interdependence, 25-27, 33, 40-41; Non-delegable, 33, 46-47

Cronin, Thomas E., 18, 75, 99, 101, 108; Congressional-presidential relationships, 19; Presidential public image, 15, 21; White House cabinet separation, 8, 17, 20, 71, 100

Cummings, Milton C., 75, 98, 99, 100, 109

Dahl, Robert A., 99

Danielson, Michael N., 75, 98, 99, 100, 109

Davis, James W., Jr., 11, 16, 17, 19

Davis, Kenneth Culp, 50, 91

Democracy, Anti-democracy at 1787 convention, 64, 85; Group process, 85-87, 99; Public participation in control processes, 1, 106; Tripartite representation, 24, 56, 57, 63; Wider scope of interest groups, 86-87, 95-96

Departmental subunits, 7-13, 71, 84, 91, 93-96

Diamond, Martin, 97, 109

Dixon, Robert G., Jr., 52

Doig, Jameson W., 17

Dolbeare, Kenneth W., 99, 109; Elitism, 99

Dry, Murray, 26

Dunn, Charles W., 20, 59

Dye, Thomas R., 75, 100, 110; Elitism, 99

Easton, David, 75

Ebenstein, William C., 75, 77, 99, 110

Edelman, Murray J., 99, 109; Political symbolism, 21

Edwards, David V., 108

Egger, Rowland; Bureaucratic separation, 5, 10-11; Statutory source of departmental power, 67; "Triple alliances" 11, 101

Eisenhower, Dwight D., 20

Elitism, 76, 85, 87, 97, 99, 110; See also Democracy, Groups, Pluralism

Executive - administrative forces; Bureaucratic autonomy, 5-22, 108-117; Control of administration, 65-68, 91-96; Departmentalization, 80-82; Internal checks, 70-73; Presidential powers, 35-39; See also Appointing power, Cabinet, Departmental subunits

Executive privilege, 28, 68, 69, 93

Factions, see Groups

Fallows, James, 4

Farrand, Max, 77

Federalist Letters, see Hamilton, Madison

Fenno, Richard E., Jr., 9, 100

Fenton, John H., 112

Ferguson, John H , 110

Fisher, Louis, 20, 21

Fisk, Winston Mills, 97, 109

Ford, Gerald R., 61, 90

123

125

Morrow, William L., 12, 17, 20, 78, 94, 101

Mosca, Gaetano, 99

Mullen, William E., 8, 22

Murphy, Walter F., 75, 98, 99, 100, 109

Musolf, Lloyd D., 112

Mutual deference, 84, 88

Mutual negative, 56-57, 58, 64, 69, 75, 76, 94

Nanda, Krish, 116

Nathan, Richard P., 20

Neustadt, Richard E.; Administrative identity, 9, 71; Executive Office, 18; Presidential limitations, 10, 16, 90; Shared functions, 59, 60; Subcommittees, 83, 88

Nimmo, Dan, 75

Nixon, Richard M., 28, 61, 77, 90, 106, 110

O'Connor, Robert E., 114

Ogden, Daniel M., Jr., 111

Ogul, Morris, 50

Olson, David J., 97, 99, 114

Palumbo, Dennis J., 75, 114

Parenti, Michael, 99, 114

Pareto, Vilfredo, 99

Parthemos, George S., 99, 100; Control of bureaucracy, 110

Paterson, William 32

Peek, George A., Jr., 74

Peltason, J.W., 75, 99, 108

Permanent government, 5-8, 13-16, 19-21, 47, 70-73, 91, 110

Peters, Charles, 4

Plamanetz, John, 74

Plano, Jack C., 76

Plato, 56, 74

Pluralism, 63, 76, 84-87, 94, 99, 116, see also Elitism, Groups

Political appointees, 2, 6, 8, 15, 17, 20, 22, 77, 90-91, 109, 116

Polsby, Nelson E., 4, 14

Polybius, 56, 74

Pomper, Gerald W., 19

Powell, G. Bingham, Jr., 75, 97

Powers, meaning of, 24, 29

Presidential activism, 1, 2, 5, 9, 11, 14, 35-38, 55

About the Author

Henry J. Merry is a Professor Emeritus of Political Science of Purdue University, living at Ann Arbor, Michigan. He has undergraduate and law degrees from the University of Michigan and holds an M.A. in Political Science from American University, an LL.M. from Harvard University, and a Ph.D. from the London School of Economics and Political Science, University of London. Before joining the Purdue faculty he was an associate professor at Northern Illinois University. Previously, for several years, he engaged in legal work in private and public positions. His twelve years of service with the national government included two years as legal analyst with the Legislative Reference Service, Library of Congress, and five years (1947-52) as Chairman of the Excess Profits Tax Council of the Bureau of Internal Revenue. He is the author of Montesquieu's System of Natural Government, published by Purdue University Studies in 1970. His articles have appeared in the American Bar Journal, the Western Political Quarterly and the Minnesota Law Review. The American Bar Association in 1954 made him recipient of its Ross Essay Award for an essay on the Investigating Power of Congress.